Conducting Narratives

Conducting Narratives

Navigating Through Complexity Using Strategic Improvisation

Jesper Falkheimer, Hans Gennerud,
Katarina Gentzel Sandberg and Mats Tyrstrup

Routledge
Taylor & Francis Group
LONDON AND NEW YORK

DESIGNED COVER IMAGE: Mattias Gustafsson.

First published 2026
by Routledge
4 Park Square, Milton Park, Abingdon, Oxon OX14 4RN

and by Routledge
605 Third Avenue, New York, NY 10158

Routledge is an imprint of the Taylor & Francis Group, an informa business.

British Library Cataloguing-in-Publication Data
A catalogue record for this book is available from the British Library.

ISBN: 9781032554587 (hbk)
9781032554594 (pbk)
9781003430803 (ebk)

DOI: 10.4324/9781003430803

Typeset in Univers and Bembo by **ART DIRECTOR:** *Mattias Gustafsson.*
FINAL ART: *Alexandra Augustsson.* **IMAGE RETOUCH:** *Peter Lundström.*

Publisher's note: This book has been prepared from camera-ready copy provided by the authors.

CONTENTS

FOREWORD

What is required to successfully lead an organisation? For nearly thirty years, I have posed this question with increasing curiosity to the many managers I have had the privilege to work with, both in the private sector and public administration. Over the decades, the answers have evolved both in content and form. From the almost religious conviction in the early nineties regarding the salvational effect of management by objectives to today's situation, where certainty has waned and the belief in a one-size-fits-all model has faded.

Regardless of the organisation's focus, all leaders testify that their environment has become increasingly challenging to interpret and predict. In various combinations, the respondents highlight that their environment has become VUCA: *Volatile, Uncertain, Complex, and Ambiguous.* Another common perception is that the significance of co-workers on the organisation's outcomes is critical, coupled with the ability to motivate everyone to take on the tasks the organisation faces. But too often a common pattern emerges – one that contradicts management's expressed aspirations – the prevalence of uncertainty about a higher purpose, internal conflicts, and objectives that become counterproductive.

So, is there a simple way to bridge the gap between management's ambitions and co-workers' experiences? The answer is undoubtedly no! No organisational miracle cures will heal disengaged co-workers and frustrated managers. If we instead ask whether there is something we can do to improve the situation for most people, the answer is undoubtedly yes. The book you are currently holding in your hand explores possible answers to the question: What is required to successfully lead an organisation?

The Jewish author and Holocaust survivor Viktor E. Frankl writes that "the one who knows their "why" can overcome whatever "how" life presents". Starting from this seemingly simple insight, we, as the authors of this book, have set our course. What fundamentally motivates people across all contexts is what they perceive as meaningful. Formulating the purpose of an organisation and making it comprehensible is the aim of what we refer to as a narrative in this book, and its design and execution as a narrative strategy. Our conviction is that those who grasp the interplay between purpose, narrative, and motivation hold the keys to transforming not only small contexts but entire worlds... Of course, achieving lasting change requires much more, but without the trinity of purpose – narrative – motivation, our collective insight as researchers and practitioners is that no enduring transformation can occur.

In the VUCA world in which we all live, besides a strong narrative, the ability to improvise is also essential. Plans are overturned, and reality challenges control, impacting all organisations. The way to meet this challenge is by developing the skill of improvisation. And with a clear narrative, it becomes significantly easier to do so. Just as a clear musical theme allows an instrumentalist to explore new harmonies.

We hope that reading this book will help you discover new knowledge and inspire fresh insights. May you also identify your favourite instrument for improvisation.

The authors want to express their gratitude towards more inspiring people than we can mention here, who have contributed to this book in different ways – colleagues both from academia and the agency Gullers Grupp. In previous books in Swedish, we have based many of our thoughts on interviews with successful leaders in both the public, private and non-profit sectors. These interviews have been valuable input also for this book, which is being written a few years later. A special thanks to Britt-Marie Ahrnell and Arne Forsén. Oskar Kalmaru, Agitator Whisky, has contributed with his start-up world thoughts in this book, and copywriter Nina Lee has contributed with interpretation and translation of several chapters. Art Director Mattias Gustafsson has given the book its amazing graphic form.

Hans Gennerud

STOCKHOLM, JUNE 2025

“The one who knows their “why” can overcome whatever “how” life presents.”

VIKTOR E. FRANKL, HOLOCAUST SURVIVOR

CHAPTER 1

The new world disorder

Abstract

This chapter introduces the premises, aim and fundamental ideas of the book. The premise of the book is the contemporary world we live in – an increasingly interconnected world with more complex dependencies between society, organisations, and individuals than ever before. The traditional division between society and business has become obsolete while the dependencies between all institutions, actors and stakeholders create increased complexity, paradoxes, ambiguity, and constant demands of adaptation. A main question for this book is: How can the direction for an organisation's overall development be supported – as well as communicated – if planning, and even strategies, are no longer sufficient options? Our answer is – by narratives and strategic improvisation. In the chapter it is claimed that jazz music, narrative theory and improvisational theatre have more to bring to the development of organisations than traditional managerial models.

THE PREMISE FOR THIS BOOK about work, management and communication is that no organisation is an island, and that management does not happen in a vacuum. In the book we want to connect new ideas about society, organisations, and management in a framework also based in the humanities and fine arts. We combine ideas and knowledge from several fields – some very old and wise, some new and radical – to create innovative thinking. This means that we challenge established managerial ideas of an economic man, organisations as containers and society as a solid system. We believe that jazz music, narrative theory and improvisational theatre have more to bring to the development of organisations than traditional managerial models. There are several reasons for this, all somehow connected to the contemporary world we live in – an increasingly interconnected world with more complex dependencies between society, organisations, and individuals than ever before. The traditional division between society and business has indeed become obsolete. The dependencies between all institutions, actors and stakeholders create increased complexity, paradoxes, ambiguity, and constant demands of adaptation. On a systemic level, some call this a VUCA world, characterised by increasing volatility, uncertainty, complexity, and ambiguity, while social scientists name the same world *late or hyper modernity*. The consequences this creates for organisations are the starting points for this book. In this and the following chapter, we try to describe what is happening in our surrounding world of particular importance for strategic management, communications, and leadership in organisations. Because the times are a-changin'.

At the end of the following chapter, we put the light on one of the cornerstones of our thinking – narratives – and tell the narrative of narratives, as a bridge to the next chapters where we enter the world of management and organizing in time and space. These chapters aim to deepen the knowledge about these tasks from a historical approach. In these chapters – starting off in the dawn of management – the development is analysed as a triangle with changing gravity. The triangle connects the interplay between human work, the coordination of efforts by communication and the role of leadership in all of this. After these chapters, we open for a new universe for organizing, management and leadership. In this chapter we launch the concept and grand idea of *strategic improvisation*, combining ideas from management, communication, the humanities and fine arts. Strategic improvisation is an answer to the need for tools, methods, and approaches for steering organisations in our time, to be able to cope with both order and chaos, the balancing act between complexity and the changeability of everything, a clear direction and our basic needs for stability, security and common values. In the final chapter we create a synthesis of what has been written and link the ideas to a world of practice.

A point of departure for this book is the following: New ways of creating values are constantly revealing themselves and have been doing so in particular for some centuries now. However, the history of mankind may be described as a process of innovations and improvements promoting the ability to create both values and welfare. A major such change was industrialisation. A second, and very much ongoing, change is the development of knowledge work and specialist services as an expanding proportion of the economy. Our main interest is the dynamics between work, management, and communication in society, not technology as such, but the relationship between communication and digitalisation. What is said here about communication, though, naturally implies people using both digital tools and ditto channels while communicating. A theme in our analysis is concerned with the development of a VUCA world. That is, the journey towards a less predictable society. This will be analysed in this book as structurally promoted shorter and shorter time horizons applied in management. Our claim, though, is that less predictability and shorter time perspective are related. The managerial tool par excellence – the plan with a capital P – is therefore less relevant in a VUCA world. This is why the following question unfolds: How can the direction for an organisation's overall development be supported – as well as communicated – if planning, and even strategies, are no longer sufficient options? Our answer is – by narratives and strategic improvisation.

World in constant change

More than two decades years ago, the social scientist Anthony Giddens named our world a *Runaway World*, an epithet that many of us probably recognise ourselves in. A world characterised by information overload, globalisation, polarisation, experienced uncertainty, and new social formations and conflicts.

> “ We are the first generation to live in this society, whose contours we can as yet only dimly see. It is shaking up our existing ways of life, no matter where we happen to be. This is not – at least at the moment – a global order driven by collective human will. Instead, it is emerging in anarchic, haphazard, fashion, carried along with a mixture of influences. It is not settled or secure, but fraught with anxieties, as well as scarred by deep divisions. Many of us feel in the grip of the forces over which we have no power.
>
> GIDDENS 2002, P. 19

Describing the world that we live in and where it seems to be going is a magnificent task, which always entails a risk of predicting a future that no one knows much about. Describing the future also means shaping the future since trends are social constructs. When more and more people – especially those who have positions of power – tell us about what is to come, the chances that what is said will be true increase. This is the performative power of communication. That said, the grand narratives in our time are rather pessimistic, sometimes even dystopian, and quite often they lead to conflict and polarisation. It is certainly not new that many people tend to overestimate how good things were in the past and see the present as a stage of decay. It has always been said that it was better in the past, which can be questioned in all possible ways. Opinion research actually shows that people over the world are divided on whether life is better or worse.[1] People in countries such as Vietnam and India see the bright side of the future while Americans have a dark view of the future and issues such as the gap between rich and poor, political conflicts and geopolitical power position.[2] From a factual approach there is no doubt that for many people in the world there have been massive improvements in life expectancy and well-being over the last decades. But at the same time, there is undeniably justification for the pessimism due to the climate crisis and the enormous consequences this has for societies, organisations, and individuals, and due to geopolitical conflicts and the increasing threats to the decreasing number of democracies around the world.

The need for contemporary leaders to spend time to understand what is happening right now and in the future has increased. This is so since management and leadership also mean to be one step ahead in a situation with permanent changes in organisations and their environment. The ability to act upon new challenges on both macro (connected to climate crisis, inflation, geopolitical conflicts), meso (e.g. new supply chains, shortage of staff) and micro (new consumer attitudes or employee behaviours) levels is a crucial asset for professional leaders (Zerfass et al. 2023). Besides dividing trend analysis into these interconnected social levels, one may focus on three other concepts (ibid.) which are of core relevance from a communication management perspective:

SOCIETY: Trends emerging in public opinion and the public sphere which have an impact on people's trust, expectations, norms, attitudes, and behaviour (and sometimes leads to new legislation), having consequences for organisations.

MANAGEMENT: Trends in strategic organizing of management and organisational structures (such as centralisation, fusions, alliances, working methods and leadership models) which may be responses to changes in society or forced by advances in technology, managerial hypes, research, and innovations.

TECHNOLOGY: Trends in all aspects of technology (hardware, software, services) which creates new obstacles or possibilities for organisations. AI is obviously a dimension of technology having consequences that nobody can neglect.

In the next chapter, we will soon return to an attempt to describe some crucial trends in our time, which forms the premise of our proposal to embrace strategic improvisation as a new way of thinking. We start off with a more holistic approach, explaining the popular VUCA concept and how strategic improvisation is a possible answer to the challenges that VUCA creates. We also introduce the *Managerial Communication Triangle* (MC-triangle). The MC-triangle describes the interplay between human work, management, and communication in the crafting society, in industrial society and in contemporary late modern society. The MC-triangle is a framework for all our ideas and a fundament for strategic improvisation where communication (as sense-making through narratives) is on the top of the triangle. We end the following chapter with raising the importance of strategic narratives in the new VUCA world disorder and describe how narratives may be used ethically as a form of management through communication.

The main interests of this book are strategic narratives and ditto improvisation as approaches to governing organisations. As well as managing transformations beyond organisations and, thus, of the society as such. Again, time unfolds as crucial. Typically, a narrative is established over time. If not rejected or demolished by other competing narratives. However, it may also be established momentaneous as a response to a dramatic occurrence. Such as the Russian invasion of Ukraine literally changing the global world for decades to come. However, due to the compressed time perspectives in current societies, discussed in a later chapter, the need for impromptu actions has become a necessary part of strategic leadership (Falkheimer & Gentzel Sandberg 2019) matching well the leadership through everyday problem-solving, verbal communication and intuitive decision-making (Tyrstrup 2006).

Notes

1 https://www.pewresearch.org/global/2017/12/05/worldwide-people-divided-on-whether-life-today-is-better-than-in-the-past/

2 https://www.pewresearch.org/short-reads/2023/04/24/americans-take-a-dim-view-of-the-nations-future-look-more-positively-at-the-past/

References

Falkheimer, J. & Gentzel Sandberg, K. (2019). *Nu. Strategisk improvisation – ledarskap för samhällsaktörer.* Stockholm: Roos & Tegner.

Giddens, A. (2002). *Runaway World.* London: Routledge.

Tyrstrup, M. (2006). *On the Brink of Failure: The Art of Impromptu Action in Everyday Leadership.* Lund: Studentlitteratur.

Zerfass, A., Ziegele, D., Clausen, S. and Stieglitz, S. (2023). *Trend Research in Communication Management: Introducing an Interdisciplinary Approach Based on Futures Research Methodology.* paper presented at the EUPRERA 24th Annual Congress. Charles University Prague, September 2023.

CHAPTER 2

The interplay between work, management, communication in the VUCA world

Abstract

This chapter develops an overall understanding of contemporary society as well as different macro trends with consequences for management and communication in organisations. The concept VUCA, developed some decades ago, standing for volatility, uncertainty, complexity and ambiguity, is presented. Social theory on structural change is also discussed through using the concepts of late modernity and wicked problems. Some macro trends such as digitalisation, tensions between globalisation and nationalism, and crucial demands for sustainability efforts are developed. In the later part of the chapter the focus is on the relationship between society and organisations. By using the dichotomy between dominance or collaboration a model – the Managerial Communication Triangle – is presented. Three historical versions of this triangle take off from the crafting society, the industrial society and the late modern society. It is argued that sense-making communication defines our late modern societies and organisations in a world where a narrative understanding and ability for strategic improvisation are crucial.

VUCA AS A CONCEPT HAS ITS ORIGIN in the US army where it was developed in the late 1980s, based on theories developed by Warren Bennis and Burt Nanus (1985). The acronym stands for a new strategic leadership approach based in the multilateral global security context that replaced the bilateral Cold War conflict. Very soon VUCA diffused from military to general strategy scholarship, focusing on major corporate challenges of the 21st century. Among different megatrends, digitalisation and its impact on business and society is viewed as one of the core drivers of a shift toward a VUCA world. The VUCA concept has been used in different ways to understand multiple challenges. On a general level, VUCA refers to our contemporary information and communication environment, with massive floods of data and offers ideas of how to use and respond to this situation. But let us first dig more into what the acronym stands for, inspired by Bennett & Lemoine (2014).

VOLATILITY focuses on the instability in our environment – the constant movements back and forth, up and down, in a way that is hard to predict due to cascades of events. An example of this is how prices fluctuate on production and distribution of crops due to effects of the war in Ukraine and geopolitical instability.

UNCERTAINTY is a concept which is a paradoxical effect of the ever-increasing information flow – we have access to more information than ever, including new (AI) technologies that help us to create, systematise and analyse this information, but more information does not necessarily lead to certainty or common sense. In other words, we have more information, but less common meaning. More information also means more choices and increased perceptions of risk. We are expected to collect, manage, and process large amounts of information before each decision. But humans tend to prefer to reinforce what they already know, confirm their biased opinions, and avoid information that conflicts with what they know. Leaders and managers are humans, and they also prefer to confirm what they already think – and avoid negative information from other people. For managers and leaders, the flow of information is often one of the biggest problems. Lots of e-mails, constant meetings as well as new reports, investigations, surveys, analyses and strategies create a complex decision-making basis, which requires lots of time to manage. But there is less time, so decisions must be made based on the best possible interpretation, which is always uncertain.

COMPLEXITY takes its point of departure in the multiple connections between parts and variables in every situation and system, and (again) the massive volume of information that makes prediction very hard. An example of this is handling business in different societies, nations, and regions with a multitude of differing values, norms, regulations and a stream of unforeseen new events and crises.

AMBIGUITY, finally, illustrates situations where there are no simple causal relationships, only unclear relationships that sometimes are contradictory. We face more and more "wicked problems" – problems that are difficult or downright impossible to solve, with no clear definitions, and no standardised method to follow, and often with several explanations. The idea of "wicked problems" is a good example of an old concept that is exceptionally useful for understanding the challenges of our time. The concept was coined already in the 1960s in the field of social planning by urban planner Horst Rittel. The communication scholar Jeffrey Conklin (2006) explains some decades later that a wicked problem:

1. Is not really understood until after a solution is in place.
2. Has no stopping rule – there is no traditional start, middle, and end.
3. Has no right or wrong solutions, only better or worse.
4. Is essentially unique and novel.
5. Can only be solved as a "one-shot operation".
6. Has no given alternative solutions.

Typical wicked and ambiguous problems arise when institutions and actors try to handle sustainability problems which require large efforts, multiple but coordinated strategies, and collaboration at systemic level. But wicked problems also occur in organisational decision-making and strategy formulation. We confront more and more ambiguity in our multivocal and complex environment, where traditional and linear explanations, interpretations and simple solutions do not work anymore. There is not an easy and rational way out for organisations in a world of wicked problems. The management scholars Scherer, Palazzo and Seidl (2013) conclude that societal complexity must be met with corporate complexity. This means that contemporary organisations need to adapt to the complexity and develop diverse strategies that are applied at the same time:

> There may even be a situation where a company is facing a multitude of sustainability issues and contradicting societal expectations simultaneously. Thus, the corporation might be required to manipulate the societal environment, to adapt to social expectations, and to engage in stakeholder dialogues at the same time. The challenge, here, will be to balance the inherent contradictions between these strategies and their organisational prerequisites in order not to lose trust and credibility and, thus, legitimacy.
>
> SCHERER, PALAZZO AND SEIDL 2013, P. 271

Analysing complexity using time

Complexity has a special position in the VUCA definition. For the simple reason that the term refers to actual structures and processes in such a world. Volatility, uncertainty and ambiguity, on the other hand, refer to characteristics of what is existing in a VUCA world.

Several authors (e.g. Bourdieu 1982, Heilbroner 1962, Wallerstein 2004) have suggested time to be a fundamental dimension when analysing social as well as societal complexity. The typical claim is that complexity refers to the actual things or phenomenon in the world as well as a multitude of relations among these things. Most of them unknown or at least purely understood. Things, though, tend to be more easily detected, due to being tangibles, while relations often are intangibles. Thus, an aspect of complexity – and an important part of what is defining the concept – are the many and unpredictable relations existing in an extensively interconnected world. In that sense, time can be viewed as a magnifying glass. The length of the studied time – the longitudinal dimension – multiplies the number of situations constituting the observed social system. Therefore, pattern recognition, including tendencies to interrelatedness, are facilitated.

A new social paradigm and megatrends

Which megatrends define our surrounding world? The answers depend, but the same overall global trends seem to recur in the contemporary debate. Digitalisation (now mainly focusing on AI, artificial intelligence), tensions between globalisation and nationalism, and crucial demands for sustainability efforts are examples that have been on the agenda for several years now.

In a certain sense, these macro trends are not always made concrete, and they are sometimes used without a historical framework. Already Karl Marx, for example, highlighted the power of massive globalisation, as he experienced it in the 19th century. The impact of new digital technologies, including AI, has been discussed for decades. Sustainability, as categorised in the UN Sustainability Development Goals, has indeed a shorter history in the public debate – starting off in the late 1960s – but the reasons behind climate change, human and social inequality obviously have a long history. In any case, many probably agree that new digital technologies turn a lot of things upside down, that organisations, nation states and individuals are increasingly interconnected in a global system and that organisations must take greater social, environmental, and economical responsibility. More and more people see themselves as societal actors whose decisions and actions have consequences not only for the organisation's shareholders, customers, or target groups, but for the development of society in general.

There is, as mentioned before, a general experience of *uncertainty* in the Western part of the world that keeps recurring. Several social theorists have emphasised this increasing and collective perception among humans all over the world, but perhaps especially among people that are connected to our contemporary information systems where more and more information does not lead to more certainty, but a sense of uncertainty. The only thing that is constant is the X factor, according to several leaders we have interviewed (Falkheimer & Gentzel Sandberg 2019). X is used here to denote constant change. In other words, X stands for the unknown and has been used in this way in a variety of areas throughout the ages, both in science and popular culture. For example, the Enlightenment philosopher René Descartes used X (as well as Y and Z) in his mathematical system to denote "unknown values", while the talent competition *X Factor* connects X with that little something extra that can't quite be described. As you will find out later, X is an important driver behind the idea of strategic improvisation.

In the year this book is being written – 2024 – everyone seems to be talking about AI, *artificial intelligence*, which is supposed to have huge implications for societies, organisations, and individuals. So, let's start there. Artificial intelligence means, somewhat simplified, that intelligent machines can take over tasks that were previously performed by humans. Dreams or nightmares about intelligent machines have existed throughout the ages and are already mentioned in Greek mythology, while the concept was coined in the 1950s.

AI is a large and complex scientific field that has come into the world's focus at different periods, only to return to standby and then reappear. For the public, AI was previously mainly associated with the occasions when intelligent computers won over humans in various games, which for example happened in 1997 when the chess-playing computer Deep Blue defeated the then world chess champion, Garry Kasparov. What significance AI will have for management, communications and organisations can only be predicted but there is no doubt that AI is already having a massive impact on all aspects of society and business. An expected consequence is that robotisation and automation lead to less qualified and low-paid tasks being taken over by machines. This in turn may lead to increased economic gaps but also increased efficiency. The economic divides might in turn lead to increased political polarisation and democratic challenges. Especially since AI is and will in an unprecedented way be used to produce and spread massive amounts of disinformation (e.g. deepfakes) that threaten the liberal-democratic world society. In the World Economic Forums, *Global Risks Report 2024* it is concluded that: "Misinformation and disinformation are biggest short-term risks, while extreme weather and critical change to Earth systems are greatest long-term concern."[3]

Quite another possible consequence is that human leadership becomes even more important. This is if we assume that morality and ethics are ultimately human issues and not something that can or should be delegated to machines.

Another megatrend that needs to be highlighted is the increased focus on scarcity management. For decades, people in the rich part of the world have lived in an excess of goods and services. But times are changing. The Covid-19 pandemic and Russian war in Ukraine are two of the driving forces behind the increase of scarcity and bottlenecks. Even bigger reasons for this trend are the demographic challenges (shortage of working staff and competences, increase of senior citizens and a mismatch at the labour market) and the dwindling nature resources (the climate and energy crises). Steering organisations in a world of scarcity is something quite new, perhaps not if we look back over several decades, but if we only look back at the last. This development – delays, shortages, bottlenecks – is challenging for organisations and increases the need for flexible and improvisational solutions. On the one hand, waiting for a product or a service may raise the consumers' interest; this psychological mechanism (the risk of losing something triggers behaviour) is well-researched in behavioural economics and used all the time by marketers. On the other hand, delays and shortage can of course lead to negative emotions, criticism, and bad organisational reputation. But fundamentally this is an also a matter of sustainability – some forms of mass production and mass consumption are not sustainable for our world and perhaps scarcity is something that organisations need to integrate into their business models instead of confronting it.

Are we then living in an era of me, myself and I, a narcissistic culture where the individual comes first and the collective last? This might be a bit overstated since individualism is a fundamental driver of Western modern society since the 18th century or so. But during the earlier phase of modern society, individualisation was primarily about the individual's rights in relation to the state and other authorities. In our time, individualisation can be assumed to be more about people being expected to take personal responsibility, make their own choices, and not rely on collectives, authorities, or traditions. This movement has also been going on for a long time. The French philosopher Jean-Paul Sartre, a prominent figure in the Existentialist movement that emerged after the Second World War, stated that we are "doomed to freedom", which creates anxiety for modern man. From an organisational perspective, one can perhaps be less philosophical and state that the leaders of our time must deal with employees and customers who want to be treated as individuals rather than functions or numbers. Involvement in collective movements or groups persists in many contexts but is weaker than in the past. Member organisations based on collective core values are forced to adapt and individualise their operations; if you become a member with us, you get a discount, free insurance, individual feedback etcetera! Managers and leaders in other organisations are expected to give individual feedback on the employees' efforts and are also assessed as individuals themselves. To reach out to and create relationships with customers, citizens or other stakeholders, increasingly individualised and adapted communication is needed. Which in turn means that tech giants such as TikTok, Google or Facebook have ended up in the centre as they have collected large amounts of information about each user (and offer this to keen speculators). Parallel and perhaps paradoxically with the individualisation in its various forms, there is an increased "dividualisation" made possible through new communication platforms. By dividualisation is meant the increased sharing and spread of communication that takes place, for example, within social media platforms – an individual post can, if it is attractive, be shared many times. The possibilities for dissemination are immense, but it is not a new world that has arisen – the principles for what is valued as interesting news are probably quite similar. Famous people's posts are shared significantly more than unknown people's, for example.

So, are we in a paradigm shift where a completely new social structure replaces the old one? Where everything old is passé and the new completely takes over? Doubtful, many would say. Prominent social scientists such as Anthony Giddens, Zygmunt Bauman and Ulrich Beck think or thought a little differently, but all emphasise that we rather live in a hypermodern or late modern world where the traits of modern society are still fundamental. Since a few hundred years ago, we in the developed part of the world have lived in the era of modern society. Some Western countries are based on principles of modernity regarding individual rights, sensible social solutions while religion has been relegated to the private sphere. According to the World Values Survey, which measures cultural value systems in different countries, there are two axes that different countries place themselves on: individualism or collectivism, and secular-rational or traditional-religious values.[4] This division is challenged though, since different groups of people in globalised societies often live side by side in nation states – sometimes in harmony, but often in increased conflict (regarding values, culture, and norms). This late modern and VUCA world is a consequence of modern society. The strong modern faith in technological and scientific progress, focusing on rights of the individual and well-planned industrial organisations, has created effects that are in some sense paradoxical.

The interplay between social change and organisations

So, what about the relationship and interface between social change and organisations? According to our understanding we need to fly high to understand the massive transformation that has taken place among contemporary organisations and business. We believe that one way of understanding what has happened and what is happening is to use one dichotomy – between *dominance or collaboration* – and a model – the *Managerial Communication Triangle* – which we have developed.

Dominance or collaboration

The trends that we highlight above are not isolated from each other but interrelated. They all define the VUCA, late modern, or wicked world order – which organisations may counter, adapt to, and try to handle differently.

One possible response is to use established methods and tools (see also later in the chapters on history of organizing and management) to keep control and dominate. This leads to an increased focus on long-term planning, dividing organisations into functions, documenting, measuring, focus on information (but not communication), and evaluating results, as well as creating new administrative tasks and systems for control. Following this logic, different models are applied to clarify which results have been achieved for individuals, employees, managers, and entire organisations. Financial results are self-evident to assess, but in our time, this is not the only thing measured – everything that may be measured will be measured as a key figure. This may sound reasonable, but also involves a lot of risks. Firstly, measurement with so-called KPIs (key performance indicators) can lead to employees become so goal-focused that they let go of all forms of critical thinking about why they work in certain ways towards certain goals. Doing things right becomes more important than doing the right things. Secondly, these measurements show results on an aggregate level and do not give a reliable view on qualitative real-life aspects. The value of a personal conversation in peace and quiet between an employee and a customer or citizen is rarely captured in a key figure. Thirdly, there is a risk that documentation, evaluation, and measurement take up so many resources that the core business itself is affected – you simply spend more time documenting, measuring, and planning than doing what you are supposed to, and lose creativity. We will come back to this later, but it may already be said that, yes, we need to analyse what we do, but should spend more resources on creating than documenting.

Slightly simplified, there are two diametrically different approaches to what is going on. Either organisations, as mentioned above, do what they can to maintain control, dominance and governance, or they accept the prevailing runaway world and do what they can to take initiatives for collaboration, aiming for developing their operations aligned with what is happening here and now. That goals are important as benchmarks for organisations goes without saying. But if the management's task is to manage in detail through goals, then it becomes a different story. The methods then will not be to paint overarching and engaging goals or narratives that also include why we need to get there, but instead to build standardised systems where everything that can be documented and counted is seen as vital to control so that everything is done correctly. In the same spirit, predetermined results, preferably defined in exact numbers, become a way of planning one's business. We can call this approach the *dominance strategy* and it is essentially based on premises from industrialism: viewing organisations as machines, people as functions and managers as authorities. When it comes to the organisation of work and activities, this means a preference for centralisation. To avoid the mess out there and create a feeling of being in control, the idea is that centralisation of functions and decision-making works best. It's not wrong per se, because centralisation can sometimes be an excellent principle for creating order and clarity. But quite often, centralisation is carried out as a method to create an illusory order while at the same time reducing commitment and the opportunity to create value at the very end of the organisations. A completely different approach that tries to align the organisations to the perceived uncertainty and paradoxes while taking strategic initiatives can be called the *collaboration strategy*. It is in this strategy that our idea on strategic improvisation takes its starting point. Instead of counteracting the runaway world around us, we embrace it and try to create innovations through new ways of collaborative working, organizing and managing. Instead of focusing on documentation, long-term planning through detailed goals and centralisation, the emphasis is on learning through mistakes, decentralisation and committed employees who drive development here and now. The idea is not to spend more resources than necessary on the organisation's administrative superstructure, but more on the action close to citizens, customers and other stakeholders or target groups. A consequence of this thinking is that organisations can act more quickly when something happens. Not based on a random logic, but because there is a good balance between clear structure (everyone knows what needs to be done and why it is done) and freedom for the employees to act freely within the existing framework. Taking one's starting point in this thinking also means placing narrative as a cornerstone in the steering of organisations. From our perspective, the ability to create or use strategic narratives is crucial for contemporary organisations.

The transformation of work, management and communication

Throughout this book a common theme is the interplay between human work – professional or non-professional – the effort to coordinate activities by communicating, and the role of leadership or perhaps management. Leadership and management are used somewhat interchangeably. However, a rule of thumb is using leadership while emphasizing the presence of people in attempts to govern the development, as opposed to management while the system aspects of governance are emphasised. Though, our model of interactions among human work, management and communication constitutes a triangle, and we need to grasp how that triangle, shown first in Figure 1 below, has altered over time, beginning with manufacturing products using craft.

The industry society emerged from innovations replacing earlier crafting with industrial manufacturing. Though, in the crafting society, human work was at the very core of welfare creation. Human work then included farming and trading of products. In Figure 1 this is illustrated by putting human work – work as craft, though – at the very top of the triangle. In crafting, whether concerned with glass blowing, forging or brick production, work was carried out in workshops. Typically, on a scale allowing everyone to personally know everyone else. Thus, these conditions made humans talking directly to each other the main form of communication to coordinate the different work activities.

THE CRAFTING SOCIETY

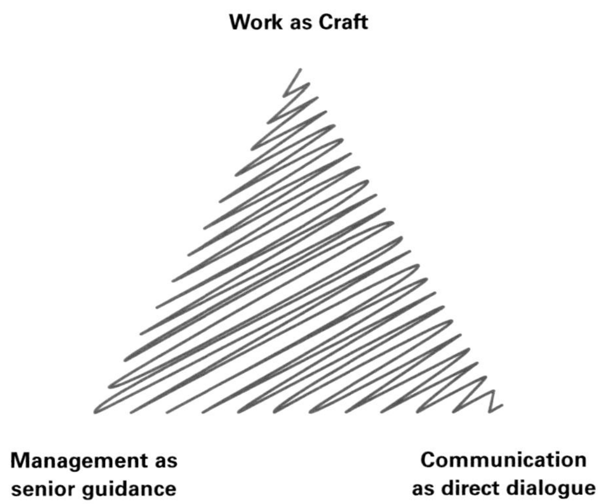

Figure 1. Human work, management and communication – Crafting.

To the extent there were needs for supervision it was done by senior craftsmen and craftswomen providing a stewardship being the masters. For example, they had to inform about what to do in terms of volumes. But less often, concerning how to do something which was an integrated part of the shared professional know-how. What might be subject to uncertainties, however, was how many glasses, tools, or bricks of different kinds? Problems were solved, of course, by talking directly to those working in the workshop; a kind of direct and face-to-face supervision of work. The interplay between human work, management and communication in the crafting society is illustrated in Figure 1 above.

One important feature of the industrialisation process was replacing manual work, crafting, with automated procedures that were managed using different kind of designed jobs. A major change in the triangle, and subject to industrialisation, was transferring the power concerned with work from craftsmen and ditto women to the management and the specialist designing jobs as well as organisations. This is why, in Figure 2, the Work as Craft has been replaced with management at the top of the triangle. Both these changes are discussed in chapter 3 along with other important changes occurring during the time of the industrial society.

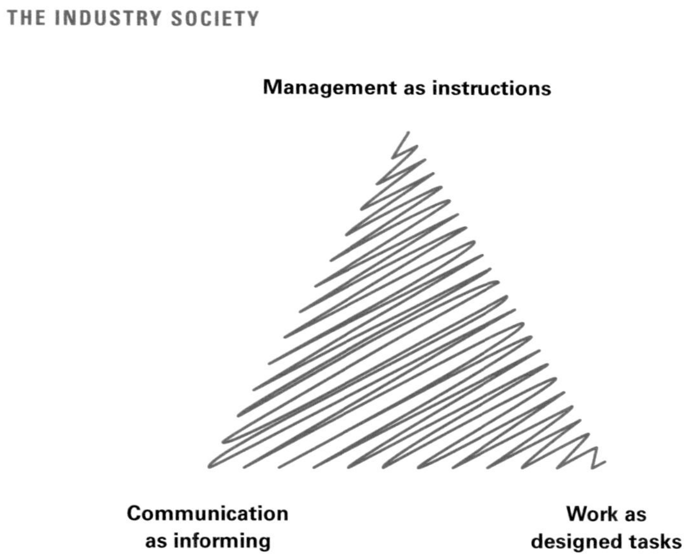

Figure 2. Human work, management and communication – Industry.

The alteration of society – from industry to knowledge work and specialist services – is also the transformation of a complicated society into a complex one, implying a general decrease in terms of predictability. This change is due to the interconnectedness of two aspects. First, the successive reduction of the relative number of relations anchored in causalities. Second, the increase of the relative number of social relations in the society. Thus, the society as a system consisting of units (people, organisations etcetera) and relations among units. In a sense, this reflects the very change in production – from products towards more of services and, therefore, activities attached to people's behaviours and lifestyles. A consequence of both a growing population – more people as well as more and more interconnected – and hugely increased opportunities to communicate. Rather, constant change, and even ongoing turmoil, reveal a growing need for impromptu actions. And this, within a context of intense and unstructured flows of information. Making the traditionally most essential tools in management – the plan with a capital P – less and less useful.

Our imaginary triangle (Figure 3 below) – as it might be described currently – is related to the maturing expert society. A society that has successively exposed itself during the past 30 years with more and more people involved in knowledge work. Our claim, though, is that communication has become an integral part of contemporary human knowledge work and specialist services. New opportunities to communicate radically have changed people's awareness of what is going on in general as well as among those they are following in social media. A main feature of the development in social sciences during the past hundred years or so has to do with an increased recognition of subjectivity and its implication. This makes a plausible "model of humans" as beings constantly understanding the world by interpreting information reaching them – communication as sense-making.

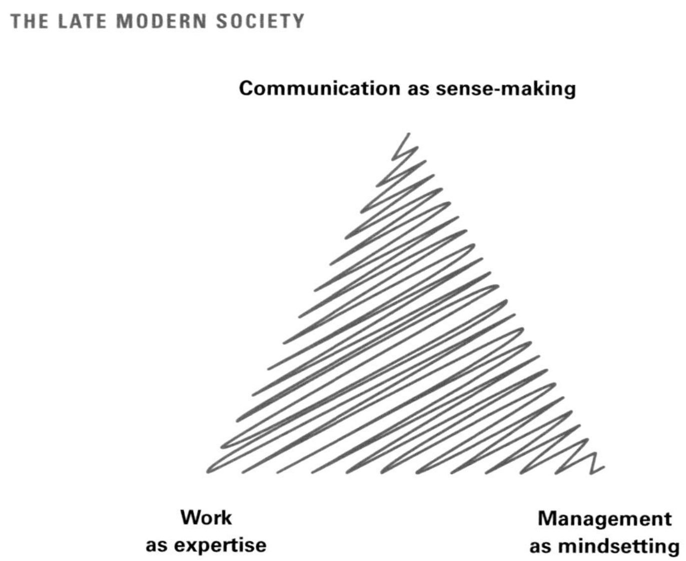

Figure 3. Human work, management and communication – Late modernity.

Thus, in our triangle model, communication is placed at the very top, recognizing communication as the very foundation of social universes. Communication creates the dimensions of the social world including the social atmospheres or ditto environments in which we find ourselves and our existences. Making leadership, in the ways we recognise it by attributing it to certain people or processes, must be interpreted to become socially real and accepted as a social reality. And fulfilling the turn of the triangle, we are back to human work this time, though, at the left corner. This is so due to the communicative aspects of knowledge work and specialist services (which will be discussed in Chapter 4). Instead of a triangle we may very well describe the evolution of three, however interrelated, fundamental processes of transformation. These are:

TRANSFORMING HUMAN WORK – from Craft to designed Jobs followed by Knowledge work & Expert Services.

TRANSFORMING MANAGEMENT – from Stewardship (direct leadership) to Management (indirect leadership) followed by Interpreting the Leadership.

TRANSFORMING COMMUNICATION – from Talking to Information followed by Sense-making.

We believe that the sense-making communication that defines contemporary societies and organisations is a world where a narrative understanding and ability for strategic improvisation are crucial.

Notes

[3] https://www.weforum.org/publications/global-risks-report-2024/

[4] https://www.worldvaluessurvey.org/wvs.jsp/

References

Bennett, N. & Lemoine, J. (2014). *What VUCA Really Means for You.* Harvard Business Review, January–February.

Bennis, W. & Nanus, B. (1985). *Leaders: The Strategies for Taking Charge.* New York: Harper & Row.

Bourdieu, P. (1982). *Habitus and Field.* Oxford: Blackwell.

Conklin, J. (2006). *Dialogue mapping: building shared understanding of wicked problems.* Chichester, England: Wiley.

Falkheimer, J. & Gentzel Sandberg, K. (2019). *Nu. Strategisk improvisation – ledarskap för samhällsaktörer.* Stockholm: Roos & Tegner.

Heilbroner, R. (1962). *The making of economic society.* Englewood Cliffs, N.J.: Prentice-Hall.

Scherer, A.G., Palazzo, G., & Seidl, D. (2013). *Managing legitimacy in complex and heterogeneous environments: Sustainable development in a globalized world.* Journal of Management Studies, 50(2), pp. 259–84.

Wallerstein, I. (2004). *World-Systems Analysis – an Introduction.* Durham: Duke University Press Books.

World Economic Forum (2024). *The Global Risk Reports 2024.* 19th ed. Switzerland.

STORY

Any old map will do

ALBERT SZENT-GYÖRGYI, WHO IN 1937 received the Nobel Prize in Medicine for discovering vitamin C, was a soldier in the First World War. He is said to have witnessed an event which has since been retold and interpreted as an example of the importance of plans, strategies, and leadership in the actual reality.

The anecdote was first made public in the early 1970s by a researcher who heard it from Szent-Györgyi. It gained further exposure through a poem by Miroslav Holub in the *Times Literary Supplement* and was later widely disseminated by organisational researcher Karl E. Weick.

A group of Hungarian soldiers was in the Alps during the First World War when their commander sent out a small group to reconnoitre the terrain. They were caught in a blizzard that lasted two days, leading the commander to regret his decision and fear for their survival. But suddenly, on the third day, the soldiers returned to camp. When asked about their whereabouts and how they managed to return, the leader of the small group explained their conviction that they would perish in the wilderness and die – until one soldier found a map in his bag. Now they knew they were saved, and after waiting out the storm they navigated back to base camp. Intrigued, the officer requested to see the map, only to discover that it depicted not the Alps, but the Pyrenees.

The story can be interpreted in different ways but has often been used in organisational research as an illustration that what is written in plans and strategies is not always so important. The main characteristics of the plan, strategy, and leadership are to create a common understanding about the overall direction and evoke a sense of security – which in turn enables action.

CHAPTER 3

The narrative of narratives

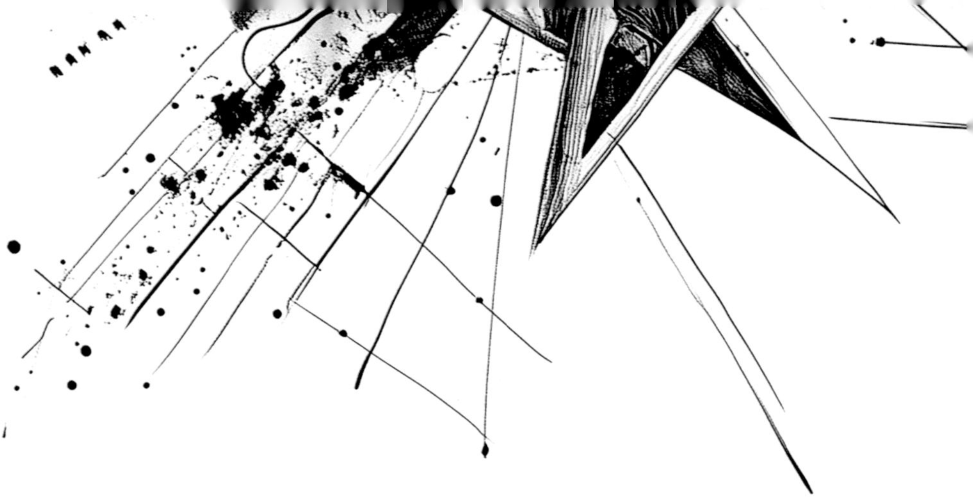

Abstract

The narrative is one of the core dimensions of the strategic improvisation concept, and in this chapter, the aim is to explain why narrative is so important for management in the contemporary complex world. Narrative theory is explained as well as different traditions about narratives as plot, structures and sense-making devices. Concrete advice on organisational and managerial narratives and storytelling is given, focusing on deep understanding, simplicity, honouring the past, clearness and forward-orientation. The definition and role of strategic narratives is highlighted. Strategic narratives are especially connected to public diplomacy, statecraft, international conflicts, and war. The importance of strategic narratives is discussed in the light of increasing spread and impact of propaganda and disinformation. Finally, so-called mini-narratives at digital platforms, challenging traditional one-way vertical narrative communication structures, are described.

SINCE DECADES AGO, the concept of brand (and branding) has dominated the organisational, marketing, and managerial discourse. A brand is usually defined as a set of tangible and intangible attributes designed to create awareness and identity and to build the reputation of a product, service, person, place, or organisation. A brand creates shared meaning and identity through communicative means and is distinguishable to other alternatives. But since the 2010s we have witnessed the rise of another concept, narrative, with some similarities to brands, but founded in a more fundamental thinking about human meaning-making, and with a much longer history in literature and fine arts. Narratives are aligned with storytelling as a practice. But often, the concept of narrative is used without deep reflection on what it means. The narrative is one of the core dimensions of the strategic improvisation concept, and in this chapter, we aim to explain why narrative is so important for management in the contemporary complex world.

Most definitions view narrative as a story of events and experiences, true or false, with an internal structure, called a plot. The philosopher and rhetoric Kenneth Burke (1969) meant that a narrative demands certain ingredients: an actor, an action, a goal, a scene and an instrument. Narratives connect the dots, link cause to effect, and create images of reality. The plot is, at least according to one research tradition, the core of a narrative, and consists of a beginning, middle and an end. It is the plot that connects all the episodes of a story, creates a meaningful whole and gives the story meaning (Murray 2003, p. 98). One of the most well-known narratologists, the Russian Vladimir Propp (1968), analysed fairy-tales and proposed that all narratives build on 31 different narrative functions connected to seven alternative characters: the villain, the donor, the helper, the princess, the dispatcher, the hero, and the false hero. Other narratologists have continued this research and found several other basic plots, such as rags to riches, the quest, voyage and return, and wretched excess. The basic idea is that all stories are constructed through a few established plots. This structuralist tradition (defining narrative structures that are universal) and assumption has been challenged since then from a so-called post-structuralist perspective. Without digging too deep into this academic field, one can conclude that later research has highlighted that we live in a world where long, complete, and fixed structure narratives are challenged by communication that happens in everyday conversation and social media interactions which may not be linked to the established narratives and plots (Dayter 2015). Digital narratives tend to be incomplete, fragmented and not following any linear logic at all.

Narratives are existential for us as humans. The narratives and plots are used by us all, trying to understand and communicate who we are. Donald E. Polkinghorne, pioneer in narrative psychology, stated that:

> Experience is meaningful and human behaviour is generated from and informed by this meaningfulness. [...] Narrative meaning is a cognitive process that organises human experiences into temporally meaningful episodes.
>
> POLKINGHORNE 1988, P. 1

Organisational and managerial narratives

Narratives are also used for organisational objectives, sometimes connected to the history and origin of a corporation, sometimes focusing strategies for the future. Narratives may be fully visible, as in corporate presentations or other forms of communications. Narratives may also be more hidden and communicated in organisational culture, everyday life, values, and performances. Organisational scholars Stefanie Reissner and Victoria Pagan (2013) make a division between two types of narrative. First, the big narrative which is typically linear and carefully crafted with a clear beginning, middle and end. Second, a minor narrative, which is fragmented and improvised and created in everyday organisational small talk. Organisational scholar Barbara Czarniawska (2004, p. 10) concluded that:

> Managers and their subordinates tell stories and write stories [...]. Narration is a common mode of communication. People tell stories to entertain, to teach and to learn, to ask for an interpretation and to give one.
>
> CZARNIAWSKA 2004 P. 10

This means that narratives and storytelling in organisations are taking place in a complex context where top-down narratives (typically implementations of strategy and other management acts) are competing with a variety of minor narratives on the floor (related to everyday work, trust, and former experiences).

Harvard cognitive psychologist Jerome Bruner (1987) concluded many years ago that stories are more efficient as management and leadership tools than pure facts. Facts integrated in a story are 22-times more memorable than if told alone, he claimed. Forbes journalist Adrian Dearnell (2021)[5] suggests that corporate stories and narratives also need to be audited, managed, and developed. The corporate narrative must be grounded in corporate history, mission, and actions, but in alignment with socio-political and cultural shifts in the surrounding society. Dearnell highlights the trends towards corporate citizenship (from CSR to Corporate Social Advocacy) and a need for a clear and legitimate purpose as relevant parts to integrate in contemporary corporate narratives.

Harvard professor Frances Frei and entrepreneur Anne Morriss (2023, pp. 62-71) give further and concrete advice on how to optimise the effect of storytelling for change management:

UNDERSTAND DEEPLY, DESCRIBE SIMPLY: If you want people to pay attention to and get interested in a planned process, you need to formulate it as a compelling, authentic, and clear story.

HONOUR YOUR PAST: Even if there is a clear future focus, you need to pay respect to the history and past. Communicating that everything is a disaster in the current organisation, and that the proposed change will turn this totally around easily creates opposition among co-workers with a long history in the corporation. Reality is seldom black and white, so you need to also "acknowledge the good parts of your history" (ibid., p. 66).

PROVIDE A CLEAR AND COMPELLING MANDATE FOR CHANGE: The mandate is only given to you if you can answer why a change process must start. This may be obvious for the C-suite, but not at all for managers and co-workers. In fact, this part of the storytelling is often a weak spot – the management explains how and where but neglects the main why question.

DESCRIBE A RIGOROUS AND OPTIMISTIC WAY FORWARD: The plan needs to be directed towards a clear and understandable goal, and the management needs to create enthusiasm among co-workers. If possible, the process may also be divided into chapters, with milestones that are celebrated when reached.

PUT THE PIECES OF YOUR STORY TOGETHER: The media is the message, as media scholar Marshall McLuhan once wrote. The story needs to be communicated in different channels and through diverse platforms, but still be coherent. The implementation of a change process as a story is a complex journey that may include personal meetings and dialogues, hearings, events, visual communication, leaflets, digital products and so forth.

REPEAT YOURSELF. If one wants the story to have an impact it needs to be repeated in all possible situations and contexts. As a communicator/manager one may get bored by hearing oneself repeating the same story, but it is necessary to get through to people.

IDENTIFY AND USE YOUR EMOTIONS. This advice may sound simple, but many change processes in organisations are communicated mainly using rational argumentation or logos as it is called in rhetoric. Stories that have an impact on people's opinions and behaviour need to raise emotions and cannot only by focused on rational and causal explanations.

Strategic narratives

The managerial approach to narratives mentioned above is not new, but has a renaissance, sometimes as "storytelling" and sometimes in a new dress named "strategic narratives". This concept is especially connected to public diplomacy, statecraft, international conflicts, and war. In a world of increasing spread and impact of propaganda and disinformation, the role of strategic narratives is getting more important. Ekman and Nilsson (2023) describe, as a valid example, how Ukraine and its president Volodymyr Zelensky use strategic narratives to create resistance towards the aggressor Russia. The strategic narrative directed to the Ukrainian people has focused on morale and resilience and never giving up:

> “This has contributed to strengthening the image of Zelensky and the Ukrainian nation as an underdog, that this is a story of a Goliath-like belligerent attacking an underestimated David.
>
> EKMAN AND NILSSON 2023, P. 30

The aligned strategic narrative towards the international and Western community emphasise that Ukraine's cause is universal and if Russia is not stopped, they threaten the whole democratic world order, and that the people of Ukraine are fighting for all of us. This narrative is also supported by the nation branding campaign with the main message "Be Brave Like Ukraine" that was launched in 2022.

According to De Graaf et al. (2015, p. 9) a strong strategic narrative is characterised by four elements.

CLARITY OF PURPOSE: This means that actors should avoid complex and ambiguous narratives and instead try to make them easy to understand, preferably with clear answers to "why" connected to current values and perceptions among the people. A purpose that may be connected to a narrative of good and evil, or good or bad, is obviously more effective if it is authentic.

PROSPECT OF SUCCESS: People support narratives that tells us that it is possible to reach the overall goal. If reality is dark and the mission seems impossible, the support for an actor goes down. In a corporate setting this means that tactics that visualise that the organisation is on the right way ahead can be used, to create new energy for moving further.

CONSISTENCY: Coherency and consistency are necessary for narratives that aim to be strategic. In political communication it is often recommended to "stick to the message" for the same reasons – to get impact there is need of repetition, and for credibility people need to know that you really believe in what you communicate.

ABSENCE OF COMPETING NARRATIVES: In conflict situations there are always competing narratives, but an actor may at least try to avoid competing narratives in their own domain. Basically, it is better for many organisations to collaborate and try to align to the same strategic narrative than to create several different ones.

Digital and participatory narratives in flux

The idea of a strategic narrative that persuades an opinion or group is fascinating, but also simplified since it describes communication as a one-way and linear process. Narratives in our VUCA world – in societies as well as in organisations – rarely just travel top-down or from a centre to a periphery. Instead, narratives are continuously in flux and co-produced by diverse actors in a multi-vocal arena. Strategic narratives launched by management in a corporation may be embraced by co-workers and stakeholders as well as opposed and rejected. If the strategic narratives mirror values and images that are grounded in and outside the organisation, the opposition will be minor, but there is usually never a unanimous support from all parties. Digital platforms and channels create both opportunities and obstacles for strategic narratives. Narratives are not fixed entities that enter social media platforms. Strategic narratives created by corporations may be contested when reaching social media actors, which are not recipients but co-tellers of narratives. The participatory nature of contemporary digital platforms has challenged the traditional one-way mass communication model and has the potential to lead to increased openness, participation and dialogue (or multilogue due to the openness). Narratives are created in a participatory mode which creates more engagement, less control from established actors and risks of spreading mis- and disinformation (Page 2018, 2021). Narratives in social media can be called mini-narratives – they are small, incomplete and fragmentary. Usually, these narratives are about current affairs and ongoing events. A typical example is a crisis where many differing mini-narratives are shared in a very complex information environment, where the traditionally dominant actors (government, corporations, news media professionals) compete with myriads of individuals and self-organised groups. In this participatory environment, there are primary tellers of narratives and co-narrators, which are active in different ways – from liking, sharing, commenting to developing the "first narrative" into something quite different, sometimes by using irony, satire or parody.

Note

5 https://www.forbes.com/sites/adriandearnell/2021/01/21/is-it-time-to-reset-your-corporate-narrative/?sh=557e8194350

References

Bruner, J. (1986). *Actual minds, possible worlds.* Cambridge/MA: Harvard University Press.

Czarniawska, B. (2004). *Narratives in social science research.* London: Sage.

Dayter, D. (2015). *Small stories and extended narratives on Twitter.* Discourse, Context & Media, Vol. 10, pp. 19–26.

De Graaf, B., Dimitru, G., Ringsmose, J., Eds (2015). *Strategic Narratives, Public Opinion, and War. Winning Domestic Support for the Afghan War.* New York: Routledge.

Ekman, I. & Nilsson, P-E. (2023). *Ukraine's Information Front – Strategic Communication during Russia's Full-Scale Invasion of Ukraine.* Report FOI-R--5451–SE. Totalförsvarets Forskningsinstitut.

Frei, F. & Morriss, A. (2023). *Storytelling that drives bold change.* Harvard Business Review, No. 6, November–December, pp. 62–71.

Murray, M. (2003). *Narrative Psychology and Narrative Analysis.* In: Camic, P.M., Rhodes, J.E. and Yardley, L., Eds., Qualitative Research in Psychology. American Psychological Association, Washington DC, pp. 95–112.

Page, R. (2018). *Narratives online: Shared stories in social media.* Cambridge University Press.

Page, R. (2021). *Co-tellership in social media storytelling.* In P. Dawson & M. Makela (Eds.), The Routledge companion to narrative theory. Routledge, pp. 119–33.

Polkinghorne, D. (1988). *Narrative knowing and the human sciences.* New York: State University of New York Press.

Propp, V. (1968). *Morphology of the Folk Tale.* University of Texas Press.

Reissner, S. and Pagan, V. (2013). *Storytelling in management practice: dynamics and implications.* Abingdon: Routledge.

CHAPTER 4

The dawn of modern management

Abstract

This chapter aims to tell the history of modern management taking the point of departure in the process of early industrialisation. That is, turning craft and manual labour by professionals, into narrowly specialised tasks in designed organisations including the assembly line and the reliance on extensive centralisation. Industrialisation is understood as a governance model moving power from craftsmen and craftswomen in daily operations to line managers and specialists on designing jobs as well as organisations, with implications, of course, for communication within organisations as well as the content of managerial leadership. It is concluded that industrialisation, extensively relying on technology and technological innovations, fundamentally redefined the relations between human work, management and communication. If one wants to understand contemporary management ideas, based in the knowledge- and service-based economy, there is need of a historical understanding.

FOR SOME TIME NOW, we claim, certain values related to the development of the VUCA world are increasingly being demanded as well as debated in society. It concerns such values that can only be created by stakeholders operating jointly and in a non-linear, non-hierarchical and extensively self-organised way. Values such as human well-being, citizens' safety, and social as well as environment sustainability. However, also values like positive outcomes of fighting segregation, poverty and internationally organised crime. These values are all related to human behaviours, beliefs and experiences and therefore, shaped and established, in and by interpersonal communication as well as coordinated activities and actions. Values that are provided by societal actors either acting individually or in collaborations, however focusing on societal transformation. Many of these values cannot be supplied easily by markets and/or single organisations. And yet, people are more than willing to pay for them. The question, though, is paying how much, to whom and based on what?

Our point of departure – towards the delivery of such new values or services – is the process of early industrialisation. That is, turning craft and manual labour by professionals, into narrowly specialised tasks in designed organisations, including the assembly line and the reliance on extensive centralisation. Industrialisation led to a governance model moving power from craftsmen and craftswomen in daily operations to line managers and specialists on designing jobs as well as organisations, with implications, of course, for communication within organisations as well as the content of managerial leadership.

A decade into the 20th century, Scientific Management was introduced as the first systemised idea about the work and responsibilities of managers with a focus on productivity based on detailed time-motion studies. Studies used for designing jobs and overall organisations were guided by the norm of a constantly increased efficiency. The later development of a Human Relation School of organisations alerted practitioners, and a growing number of management scholars, to the interpersonal aspects of organisations. Thus, phenomenon such as group dynamics, decision-making procedures and motivation and incentives became core issues, being analysed to further develop a toolbox for management and efficient approaches to managing. And again, changing the triangle of human work, organisational communication and management. Revealing needs of communicating externally are recognised early in the process of industrialisation covering areas such as advertising and public relations. A system view of organisations alerted managers not only to internal communications but communicating with a variety of external stakeholders as well. Along with the necessity to make a distinction between (internal) efficiency and (external) effectiveness.

Industrialisation – work, scale, and organisations

Historically, welfare always has relied on products and services made by humans. First as collaborating groups of hunters as well as gatherers. Later as farmers cultivating the soil and always supported by tools enhancing human ability – a stone on a shaft or with arrows and bow. By successively specializing on different crafts, combined with trade, humans could provide for a growing population. All guided by an invisible hand as described and analysed by the Scottish moral philosopher and one of the very first economists, Adam Smith (1776).

The process of industrialisation was – at its very core – converting craft done in workshops and elsewhere into tasks executed as designed jobs within designed organisations (Braverman 1974). Designing work and organisations by dividing people into white-collar workers in offices, administrating the production, and blue-collar workers operating and serving machines in factories, and, of course, managers as well as supervisors on top of that.

All was facilitated by an organisational innovation – the assembly line. A procedure of activities transforming tasks, components, and raw material into products made by machines with clerks, as a modernised version of bookkeepers, planning and administrating the necessary activities made by humans. In factories, and around the assembly lines, workers interacted with the machines, long before man-machine interfaces became a topic.

The tasks carried out in factories may be described as compensating for the shortcomings of machines. Primarily by, for example, starting and ending production or supplying machines with raw material and components. Some workers carried out maintenance, while others, as textile workers, kept the machines on track. At the very end of the assembly line workers checked the quality of the produced products with the assignment to sort out what was considered primary quality as opposed to secondary. Others took over and moved the approved products into warehouses to be stocked pending sale and further distribution.

Knowledge and power

A general source of power is contained in knowledge or know-how (Foucault 1980). This is true for knowledge and know-how about processes of value creation. It may concern handling of tools and materials. Or the relation between chosen inputs, methods, and outputs. The latter in terms of quality among other aspects, often, however, such knowledge is tacit in nature and, thus, hard to share verbally (Polanyi 1967).

In craft, it is craftsmen and craftswomen that have the relevant knowledge and know-how and, thus, the power over value creation according to certain standards. This circumstance troubled the organisation designer Frederick Taylor (1911), business consultant with personal experience of management and the creator of the philosophy that later will be labelled Taylorism. In industrial settings, however, power originates from the managers having designed the organisation and the various tasks necessary to run the operation. However, more about Taylor in a while.

Industrialisation relocated the power over work from craftsmen and craftswomen to managers and their job designers. These managers and designers carried out the well-known, but in hindsight criticised, time-motion studies of workers (Mundel 1955). This procedure emphasises the distance between employers and their representatives – that is managers and supervisors – and those being employed as workers and clerks. The hierarchical feature of organizing was stressed, and even more pronounced in the industrial setting due to an explicit and formal vertical division of work. It is no mystery that the industrial organisation with its power distribution (e.g. Lukes 1974) dispersed as a governance model in both public and civil undertakings.

Investments and the challenge of scale

Industrialisations, extensively relying on technology and technological innovations, fundamentally redefined the relations between human work, management and communication. A pronounced example is how the number of people involved in an undertaking was related to produced volumes in each timespan or more precise – dissolved these relationships and made them circumstantial. Sometimes a doubled volume only needed a few additional people. Now and then a double volume was feasible while, at the same time, reducing the number of people involved. In craft, however, these relations are linear. Thus, the concept of scale, particularly scale of economics, is at the very core of industrial thinking. This is so due to the significance of investments and, therefore, the presence of fixed costs. In craft, the fixed costs are few and low, if any. Building factories, buying machines, and getting equipment, however, represents both fixed and semifixed costs. Utilisations directly related to the profitability of an investment, implying size to be strategic and growth the most noteworthy development trajectory.

Taylorism and Fayol's comments

In the early era of industrialisation, labour was hired on temporary contracts and to the extent that people's skills were needed. Being dismissed with immediate effect was matched by employees being able to leave by the day if someone for example offered them better pay.

In these conditions Frederick Taylor, mentioned before, saw several concerns (Taylor 1911). One was that employers depended on workers really doing their very best. Another problem was the cost of replacements when people frequently changed jobs, or were fired, and new employees had to be trained to fit a spontaneously organised operation. Taylor's kind of management was depending on continuity, as well as properly designed tasks and jobs, not the spontaneously developed crafts as well as crafting methods that existed at the time. This led to an information-approach which was produced only to instruct the workers as well as evaluate their performance, all for the benefit of increased productivity. The triangle of human work, management and communication was transformed in a fundamental way, putting management at the very top of things and reducing human work to executing designed jobs in designed organisations.

Taylor developed a method as well as philosophy that typically has been interpreted as being on the firm-owners' and entrepreneurs' side – and against the workers and yes, there are authoritarian and even elitist features in Taylor's reasoning. But he also claims, on the very first page of his magnum opus, that "profits as well as wages" will be much higher in companies that apply his approach to management. In a sense he points toward some kind of profit sharing, perhaps, mainly by paying better wages to those he called the first-class workmen.

A little-known fact is that Taylor was called to the US Senate for cross-examinations (Kanigel 1997). It concerned Taylor's suggestion, extremely obscure at the time, that permanent employment should not only be recognised but supported by labour-market law to provide the continuity in employments necessary for Taylor's methods to function well. In fact, Taylor's organisational innovation was the very key to organizing at a large scale and, thus, providing a precondition for the holy growth. Taylor introduced the method of time-motion studies and the new profession of time-study men (yes, they were men). He also introduced a new managerial structure with the line-organisation of supervisors and the staff-organisation with the organisation designers and experts. Equally important as Taylor's contributions was Henri Fayol's on overall organisation and governance (Fayol 1916/1949). Being an engineer from the mining industry, and a business leader himself, Fayol claimed that a single chain of command was necessary for efficient management, a claim made partly in debate with Taylor's line-staff model with its two sources of instructions to the workers. This created unnecessary ambiguity according to Fayol, who asks: Who is actually in charge?

Fayol's more important contribution was his in total fourteen principles providing the first general theory of organisational governance. Some were extremely contemporary such as extensive centralisation, detailed discipline, and handing out orders top-down. Others were rather foresighted, such as designed and fair compensation packages and incentive systems. Not to forget his spectacular claim that a corporate culture should be fostered – an *Esprit de corps*, which was Fayol's original expression, being a Frenchman by birth.

Early managerial communication

Orders and instructions summarise well managerial communication in early industrial settings, and of course, performance reports in the opposite direction. As work transformed from skill-based craft to executing routine task in organisations, know-how about value creation moved from the craftsmen and craftswoman to the managers and their organisation designers. Thus, centralizing decision-making in accordance with the industrial principle that a few tell the many what to do and how. Within workshops, busy with carpentry or pottery making, or perhaps glass-blowing, communication was essentially verbal and person to person. Or to put it simply, a direct and situation-aligned leadership communicated by senior craftsmen and craftswomen as a kind of stewardship. This communication focused on what to do, when and perhaps in what amounts or volumes, but less frequently about how. Instead, working with documents, such as plans and instructions, as well as the associated administration, was essential for managing industrial operations. Procedures and routines had to be distributed necessary for coordinating the operations. This was making the design of models – organisation charts, report structures, work procedures templates – an essential part of managerial work (Björkman 1978). An ongoing and circular approach was established for directing operations and evaluating their performances. The very ancestor, although manual, of the digital information systems and intranets of today's organisations.

Improvements should also be commented on how they were made and communicated to whom. In craft, progress was based on experience and trial-and-error; improving work methods was an essential part of professional identities and still is! This is also tacit knowledge, sometimes secret. It is still unknown how some masters among 18th century wooden instrument makers prepared their varnishes applied as finish on violins, violas, and cellos.

Keywords in industrial improvements were analysing and redesigning tasks. Improvements were based on quantitative data verifying if a certain method outperformed another. Thus, improvements were made by specialists, the job designers reviewing optional possibilities.

Of course, there were spontaneous learning curves also in industrial settings (e.g. Wright 1936), a parallel to improved ability in craft due to accumulated experience. However, planned change, combined with instructing and training workers and clerks, were the main approach in industries, with huge implications for both the kind of required information and how it was communicated using instructing and training as the vehicles of desired changes.

Further, in industrial settings, quantitative information dominated over qualitative. Contrary to the case in crafting. In craft, there were extensive needs to communicate nuances about for example the finish or colours of produced products. In industries it was more of either/or information to be communicated due to relying on standardisations. In crafting, however, visual demonstrations to deal with tacit knowledge (Polanyi 1967). In industries the design of routines was at the core of what employees needed to be instructed about. Typically, by written descriptions concerned with a particular change.

A defining difference, between improving craft as opposed to task execution improvements, concerns what is being improved. Task execution improvements are in the very design of a task. Regardless of who will reveal them. Improved craft, however, is equivalent to developing oneself – as a professional. Manifested in improved knowledge being possible to share without having to give anything up which explains why knowledge has to be transformed into products or services to become scarce and, therefore, possible to charge for.[6] This is unfolded also in the distinction between individual specialisation, or professions, and task specialisation relying exclusively and explicitly on job-design (Freidson 1988). This is having huge implications for the needs of swapping information as well as the ways that could be done – as well as managed.

Relations and knowledge work

During the 1920s, a professor in psychology and work-life at Harvard, Elton Mayo with colleagues, studied the Hawthorne plant in Boston, Massachusetts (Roethlisberger & Dickson 1943). The study was of correlations among productivity and physical preconditions (e.g. lighting, furnishings etcetera) as well as time-spendings (e.g. length and frequency of breaks). In General Electric, the company that owned the plant, they were disturbed by the constant declining productivity and considered closing it. However, willing to make yet another attempt. The surprising finding Mayo and colleagues revealed was that regardless of what changes were made, the productivity increased. Even when the researchers changed back to previous conditions to establish correlations. If a change in one direction increases productivity, changing in the opposite direction should, of course, decrease it. That is the very essence of what correlations are about.

It was suggested that the interest as such, shown to the workers by the researchers, explained the constant rise of productivity. Someone cared about the workers' situation and was curious about their opinions. The overall conclusion was straightforward. Organisations contained less visible, however powerful, psychological as well as social forces and processes. Leadership, though, was something else and much more than only the observable activities of managers.

The Hawthorne effect, as Mayo's finding was labelled, and although the research as such has been criticised, it has become the point of departure for a particular approach to organisational theorizing.The so-called *Human Relation School*.[7] It focuses on the interpersonal aspects of organizing including group dynamics, decision-making and communication processes.

Barnard and system emergence

Among classical books on management we find, of course, Chester Barnard's *The Functions of the Executive* (Barnard 1938). In that book Barnard, a business executive with experiences also from public administration and a passionate interest in sciences, presents a complete theory on organisations. He did so, from the point of view of coordinating collaborative efforts using a system theory perspective.[8] Barnard emphasised the need of understanding organisations as conscious, deliberate, as well as purposeful constructions, as opposed to the self-organised systems he also talked about (e.g. nature and society). Barnard introduced a theoretically critical distinction, between internal collaboration and collaborating with external stakeholders. He argued, obvious to us but an eye opener at the time, that organisations existed in an environment – with extensive consequences! The division in organisations and environments, of course, also reflects Barnard's distinction between being effective as opposed to efficient – later popularised as doing the right things, from the point of view of others, versus doing things right, from one's own perspective (e.g. Bennis & Nanus 1985).

Barnard's interest in the environment as the larger system organisations were part of was essential. In his introductory remarks to his book, he claims that:

> ... much of what we regard as reliable, foreseeable, and stable is so obviously a result of formally organised effort that it is readily believed that organised effort is normally successful, that failure of organisation is abnormal [...] But in fact [...] (w)hat are observed from day to day are the successful survivors among innumerable failures.
>
> BARNARD 1938, P. 4–5

Using just a few sentences, Barnard introduce a selection model implying stages of organisation development. Later developed into life-cycle theories of organisations (Kimberly & Miles 1980). In fact, he also anticipated – inspired by systems thinking – what later will be labelled the population ecology school of organisation theory (Hannan & Freeman 1989). Attempts to organise efforts normally fail, Barnard claims. However, occasionally they do not and therefore give us not only organisations but also know-how about organizing that may serve us in an upcoming future. At least for some time and, thus, reflected in the many trends and fashions occurring in management and organizing.

Barnard emphasised the importance of defining goals and communicating them throughout the organisation. He argued that large organisations had to be fairly decentralised in their design to function properly and, therefore, goals had to be communicated within the organisation guiding local decision-making and undertakings of action. Goals, though, serving as lighthouses in the sea large organisations represented and a substitute for direct leadership. His claim, though, one of the first explicit signs of an up-coming decentralisation movement to surface decades later.

Work, management and communication

It is a well-confirmed finding in management and leadership theory that the circumstances, often called contingencies, define the boundaries for what is efficient as well as effective in terms of influencing a social setting (Hales 1986, Yukl 1989). For example, the way of coordinating actions, while shifting from a crafting production model to an industrial version, changed the leadership from a stewardship among professional equals toward a modern management approach emphasizing hierarchy and role-differences. This was, though, expected and so was the transformation of power from craftsmen and craftswomen to managers and supervisors. The changed communication patterns, from professionals talking to each other towards structured flows of information – either from the centre to the peripheries or vice-versa – were also expected. All for the same reason – the shaping capabilities of circumstances. From a system theory point of view, however, everything is so to speak the circumstances of everything else. Which makes the analytical point of departure as well as any demarcations severely doubtful (Churchman 1968). Where is it reasonable to start tracking influencing relations, processes and directions? And where should it be ended! For the purposes here we may simplify the problem substantially. We are focusing on the relations between three areas of interest – work, management and, in particular, communication – as mutually structuring and defining parts of the work environment.

Starting with the conditions during the crafting society, the superior part was craft itself. It was the various crafts that determined the different needs of communicating what as well as between whom. By a stewardship the blanks were filled, such as what volumes, materials, colours etcetera, and doing this directly. That were the suitable leadership approach carried out by the senior persons among people sharing a profession (or having similar ones) and, in that sense, being equals. This is not the same as romanticising work and relations in the workshops of the crafting society. There were, of course, status differences as well as use of power. From time to time probably power usage that would be considered harassment today. However, insights concerning what was going in terms of work and crafting were shared as opposed to the industrial setting in which the fragmentation of work was promoted by the detailed designing of jobs and positions. So, it was the craft as such – including its methods, skills, tacit knowledge etcetera – that structured the need for leadership as well as communication among the involved. The latter, though, typically being accomplished by talking face to face and, thus, directly.

THE INDUSTRIAL CONTEXT

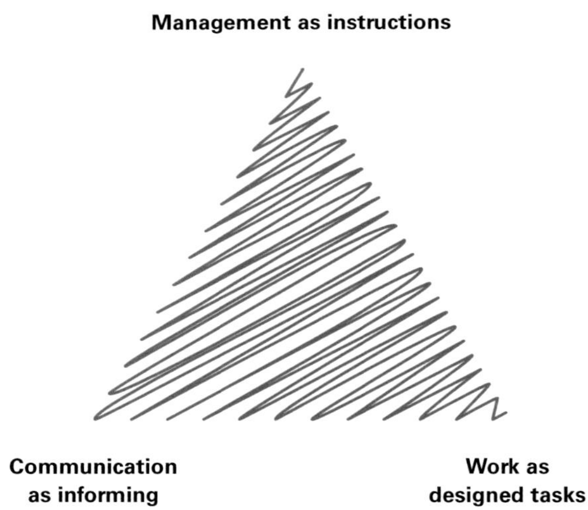

Figure 4. Managing according to the classical authors.

The process of industrialisation transformed the triangle substantially. Management became the structuring mechanism for the simple reason that it shaped the content of work. That is, by designing the tasks to be carried out by those holding a particular job or position. As prescribed! And management, as the leadership approach in use, even defined itself. Including the needs, forms and contents of necessary communication processes. Typically, though, someone informing somebody else about something job-related. Often using administrative tools such as budgeting, production plans and outcome reporting, as information vehicles. Therefore, the leadership become to a substantial part organised indirectly and interpersonal communication is reserved for those topics being too complex to standardise. Again, management as the structuring and defining mechanism.

Notes

[6] Actually, 1991 year's Nobel laureate in the economic sciences in memory of Alfred Nobel, Ronald Coase, had answered exactly that to the question "Why do firms exist?" (Coase 1937). Generalised, though, is due to transaction costs, organisations are under certain conditions more efficient than markets.

[7] Later changed to the human resource school and the immediate precursor of today's HR-departments in most organisations. Or HR-responsible in small organisations.

[8] Barnard had many friends among prominent members of the faculty at Harvard University. Thus, he spent much time discussing sciences and scientific progress.

References

Barnard, C. (1938). *The Functions of the Executive.* Cambridge, Mass.: Harvard University Press.

Bennis, W. & Nanus, B. (1985). *Leaders: The Strategies for Taking Charge.* New York: Harper & Row.

Björkman, T. (1978). *De lönsamma arbetsmiljöerna (in translation, The profitable work environments).* Sociologisk Forskning, Vol. 15, Iss. 2, pp. 11–30.

Braverman, H. (1974). *Labor and Monopoly Capital: The Degradation of Work in the Twentieth Century.* New York: Monthly Review Press.

Churchman, C. W. (1968). *The Systems Approach.* Dell Publishing Co, Ink.

Coase, R. (1937). *The Nature of the Firm.* Economica, Vol. 4, Iss. 16, pp. 386–405.

Fayol, H. (1916/1949). *General and Industrial Management.* London: Pitman Books.

Foucault, M. (1980). *Power/knowledge: selected interviews and other writings.* (eds. Gordon. C). New York: Pantheon Books.

Freidson, E. (1988). *Professional Powers: A Study of the Institutionalization of formal knowledge.* Chicago: University of Chicago Press.

Hales, C. (1986). *What do managers do? A critical review of the evidence.* Journal of Management Studies, Vol. 23, Iss. 1, pp. 88–115.

Hannan, M. & Freeman, J. (1989). *Organizational ecology.* Cambridge, Mass. Harvard University Press.

Kanigel, R. (1997). *The one best way: Frederick Winslow Taylor and the Enigma of Efficiency.* New York: Viking.

Kimberly, J. & Miles, R. (1980). *The organizational life cycle: issues in the creation, transformation and decline of organizations.* San Francisco: Jossey-Bass.

Lukes, S. (1974). *Power – a radical view.* London: British Sociological Association.

Mundel, M. (1955). *Motion and time study: principles and practice.* New York: Prentice-Hall.

Polanyi, M. (1967). *The tacit dimension.* Garden City, N.Y.: Doubleday/Anchor books.

Roethlisberger, F., & Dickson, W. (1943). *Management and the worker: an account of a research program conducted by the western electric company.* Hawthorne Works, Chicago. Cambridge, Mass. Harvard University Press.

Smith, A. (1776). *An inquiry into the nature and causes of the wealth of nations.* London: W. Strahan.

Taylor, F. (1911). *The principles of Scientific management.* New York: Harper

Wright, T. (1936). *Factors affecting the costs of airplanes.* Journal of the Aeronautical Sciences. Vol. 3, Iss. 4, pp. 122–28.

Yukl, G. (1989). *Managerial Leadership: A Review of TIneory and Research.* Journal of Management. Vol. 15, Nr. 2, pp. 251–89.

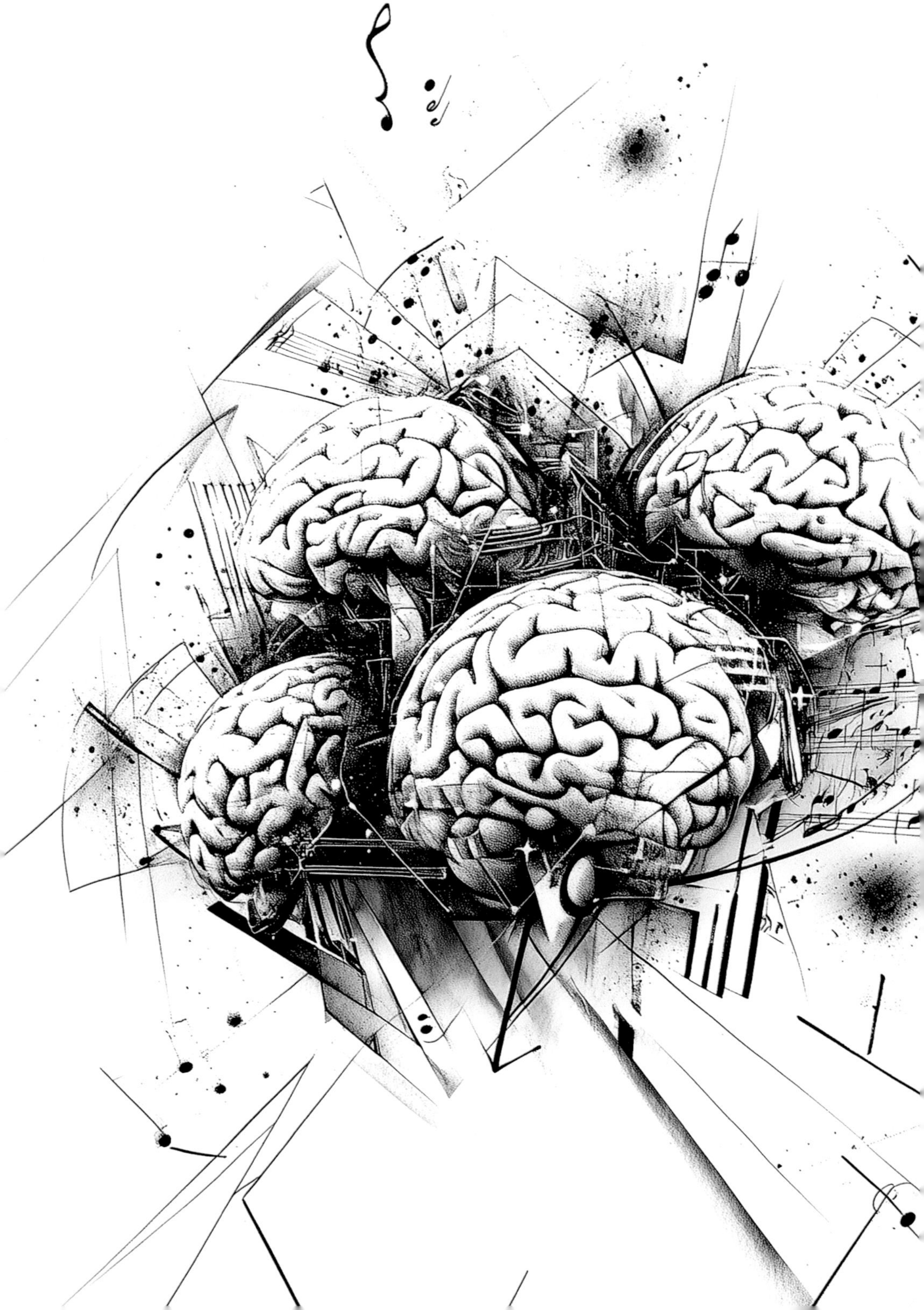

CHAPTER 5

Cognitive enterprising

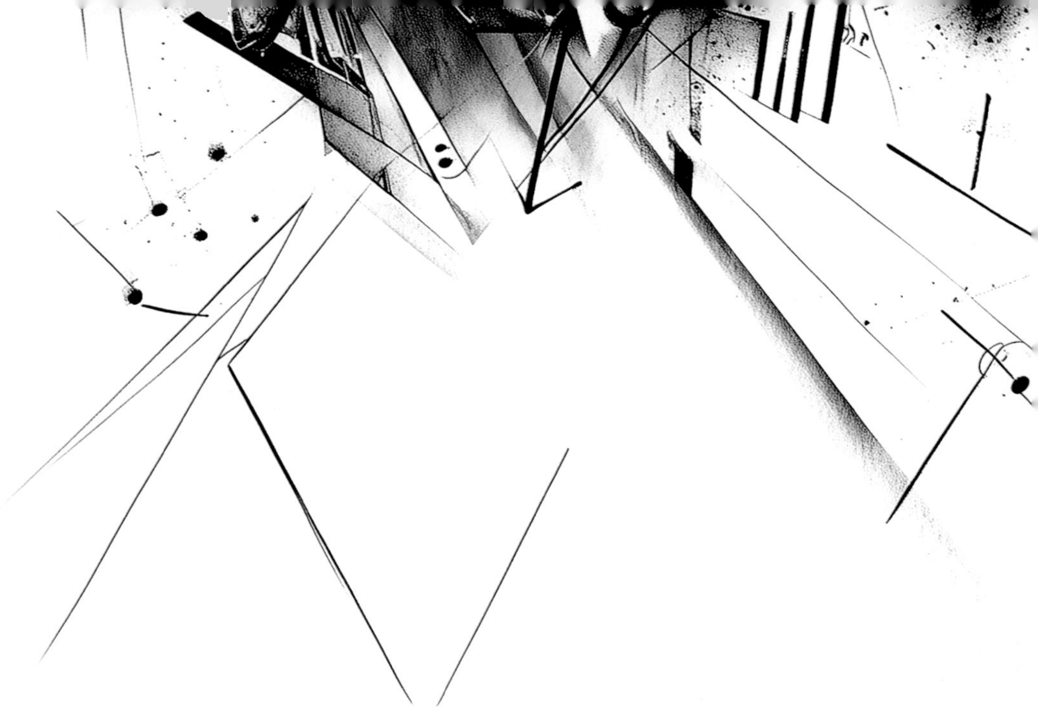

Abstract

This chapter sets the scene for the mindset that is argued for in the whole book, focusing narratives and strategic improvisation. Going back to early ideas about mental and cognitive aspects and processes in leadership and organisation, it is argued that understanding organisations from that point of view is essential for contemporary management. Organisations are according to this thinking the outcomes of socially organised processes rather than designed and implemented solutions. Accepting the claims in this chapter is putting communication at the very top of the Management Communication-triangle, introduced in the second chapter. After traveling a complete circle of the corners around it. From the down right-hand side of communicating – that is craftsmen and craftswomen talking about and organizing their assignments – passing the left-hand corner and communication as organisational flows of information – and lastly, becoming the structuring mechanism of reality.

DURING THE 1960s, and beyond, an increasing number of scholars in leadership and organisation argued that studying organisations from the point of view of mental and cognitive aspects and processes would be rewarding, with the scholar Karl Weick (1969) making a particularly important contribution. It concerned the minimum of preconditions for organised patterns, that is what we call "organisations", to emerge and become established. An emergence that had been heralded, as mentioned earlier, by Chester Barnard three decades earlier. Anchored in Weick's idea about "loose couplings" among and between activities, he had the mechanism underpinning the evolution of organised systems (of interpersonal relations or networks rather than anything else). This was a straightforward path to why Weick discussed "the social psychology of organizing" (ibid.) as opposed to designing organisations. Organizing then, being a verb, implying activities to be constitutional while organisation, being a noun, implies a planned configuration and, thus, a design as well as a designer. Weick criticised assuming organisations to be causal and in that sense machine-like in nature. Such organisations seemed to be controlled by a few – the executives – but could equally well be interpreted as an outcome of the obedience by many, recognizing, in the accepting sense of the word, of a certain set of behaviour rules to followed. Organisations are according to this thinking the outcomes of socially organised processes rather than designed and implemented solutions. Also designing organisations may be viewed as a particular and socially constructed process of organizing depending on how the processes promoting a particular design are interpreted. For example, as rational designing based on efficiency analysis or as political and socio-psychological negotiations among those having access to these processes. This being an important question from the point of view of the triangle connecting work, management and communication as one of the themes in this book.

Social constructionism

Karl Weick claimed, along with others, that the cognitive aspects of organisations had been significantly underestimated. This was the era when social constructionism (Berger & Luckmann 1966) became established in the field of social sciences and in organisation theory as well. It is reasonable to talk about a paradigm shift (Kuhn 1962) in governance reasoning, thereby opening for learning (e.g. Argyris & Schön 1978) as well as culture (e.g. Schein 1985) to simultaneously be essential features of organisations. These features imply a fundamental tension between organisational change (e.g. learning) and stability (e.g. culture); a tension that is concerned with the dynamics of organisations. If reality is fundamentally stable, then the problem becomes to explain the presence of changes and the opposite. If the world is constantly in a flux, patterns of stability must be explained. Thus, with a cognitive view on organisations a resolution was smoothly offered to why stability and change coexisted. This was done by reintroducing human behaviours and understandings as constituting components of organisations.

According to cognitive organisation theory, reality is an interpretation and, in that sense, imaginations (Weick 1969, Morgan 1986), with an emphasis on images, language and perception rather than pure imagination as fantasies. Cognitive theories claims that what we experience are interpretations and recognitions. We recognise in two senses. First, literally seeing something but also, and second, acknowledging it to be precisely that something. For example, most people may agree on seeing some flowers, however not necessarily on them being beautiful. Thus, introducing the presence of values in organisation theory and a cultural perspective on organisations (e.g., Schein 1985). Crucial for a cognitive and relational approach to leadership, is the ability to distinguish leadership from all other interpersonal aspects and influencing and establishing a social psychological understanding of leadership, which we also align with in this book. A well-known definition of social psychology, developed by the American psychologist and Harvard professor Gordon Allport, is straightforward in describing the matter. Allport argued that the discipline was occupied with "how the thought, feeling, and behaviour of individuals are influenced by the actual, imagined, or implied presence of others" (Allport 1954, p. 5).

Paul Watzlawick, an Austrian-American communication theorist and philosopher, stated in the mid twentieth century five axioms concerned with human communication. First and most important, is Watzlawick's famous claim that "one cannot not communicate". A statement that parallels Allport's "imagined, or implied presence of others", implying that we are always in a context of others no matter how physically alone we might be. The position here, though, is that we are always in social settings and, therefore, constantly involved in communication (Watzlawick et al. 1967). If nothing else, at least in a dialogue with ourselves. As cultural beings others are embedded in our "personal" norm and value systems. To put it at its extreme – we cannot be by ourselves. Yet, indeed worth noticing, this does not rule out that we might feel alone. Paradoxical as it seems, such experiences presume people belong to a social context that allows these feelings in the first place. To allude to Allport's definition – also the physical absence of others implies their existence and a lonely person being aware of this.

Drucker and the knowledge workers

A giant in the field of leadership in the 20th century, Peter Drucker, already in the 1950s proclaimed the arrival of what he called the knowledge-worker (Drucker 1959). The knowledge-workers were defined as quite different from the administrators, representatives, and clerks working in the offices at the time. Knowledge workers were well-educated, however, rarely with educations in credentialing professions – lawyers, doctors, policemen. Drucker claimed that knowledge workers would dominate a growing sector of the economy. Human recourse specialists, UX-designers and sustainability strategists are just a few arbitrarily chosen contemporary examples of representatives for what might be called the expert society (Werr & Furusten 2016) filled with knowledge workers.

In the mid 20th century, management was in the process of being professionalised. During the first decades of the century, it was noticed that the entrepreneurs, having started companies, did not necessarily manage them at a later point in time. It was called the separation of ownership and control concerning companies (Berle & Means 1932). The contours of the professional CEO unfolded. And at business schools around the world, researchers provided a successively more and more differentiated field of managerial knowledge. Today, the curriculum of a randomly chosen business school, shows a discipline truly divided into a variety of fields.

Areas such as media, well-being, finance, and education also create new professions and experts. Influencers, personal trainers, and key-note speakers are but a few examples. Digitalisation has contributed with programmers, system designers and people hosting home pages. More and more experts are adding to a growing population of knowledge workers. It is a kind of re-professionalisation of work (Duyvendak et al. 2005). Market analysis, office design and employer branding all need their own specialists. Thus, task specialisation replaced by individual specialisation. Craftsmanship is back, but also challenged by AI-services (such as chatbots or virtual influencers). However, parallel to a de-professionalisation of work (ibid.) technology reduces required know-how and replaces professionals with the less educated.

As the typographers were replaced by digital solutions in the 1970s or journalists writing directly into printing machines. Maybe AI, sensitive to likes and sharing, will replace the journalist in the ongoing fourth industrial revolution (Schwab 2016).

Knowledge work, experts, and communication

Giving orders and instructions, and demanding reports from the line-organisation, pretty much summarise the loop of management communication in early industrial companies. Two other words – representations and dialogue – do the same for knowledge work in expert societies. However, this is not restricted to managerial leadership. This is only one of four fundamental aspects of communicating within specialist services. First, to communicate using representations is a typical outcome of knowledge work. Second, the essential form of knowledge work and ditto production consists of communication. Third, outcomes of knowledge work are almost always distributed, or being delivered, by means of communication. Finally, and fourth, to communicate, using representations and dialogue, is obviously vital to managing expert undertakings and equally so in private, public, non-profit, as well as academic settings.

Outcomes of expert services – reports, events, policy documents, designs – are almost always representations or staging representations such as a management consultant presenting a three bullet-point strategy to a client, the engineering firm delivering drawings and specifications to the manufacturer of a particular kind of technical devices. An example of staging is the event bureau, performing a fashion show to present a designer's upcoming season collection. Even a decision made by a social worker concerning a client is documented and delivered in a letter or handed over during a personal meeting. This example also reveals the most fundamental communication tool of all – languages, either written (as representation) or oral (as dialogue), the latter including body language, dress-codes, and cultural signs.

However, representations and face-to-face dialogues are not only outcomes of knowledge work. A teacher discussing a subject with his or her pupils illustrates the somewhat blurry distinction between outcome (learning) and production (teaching). That is, if such a distinction is of any value? Anyhow, communicating is a crucial part also in the production of expert services.

Flipping the coin, communication is a way by which expert services are delivered and distributed. Customer meetings as well as reports are typical examples. An education program is partly produced and delivered simultaneously. The logo drawn by a design agency is mass-distributed when used for building brand awareness or corporate image. A note in the margin, but worth mentioning, is that many products are offered with some kind of expert service included. Buying an expensive bicycle is accompanied by a user manual, advising the buyer on subjects such as maintenance and troubleshooting. Applying the terminology used here, the manual is a representation of know-how about the bought bicycle. Know-how shared between a producer/constructor and a buyer/end-user, with a distributor acting as go-between.

To summarise, production, distribution, and the outcomes of knowledge work, all involve communication. Extensive communication! This is, of course, no news per se and something most people are aware of. However, it has a fundamental but less admitted implication – the relative simplicity by which a service is satisfactorily accessed and consumed is the key quality of expert services, equivalent to what sometimes is called having flow (Csikszentmihalyi 1990).

It is fair to claim that the ongoing re-professionalisation (Duyvendak et al. op. cit.) of society, moves influence and power from managers back to contemporary knowledge workers (Pfeffer 1981). Defining work – in terms of its shape, content and how to organise it – again is in the possession of craftsmen and craftswomen but those of our time – the late modern specialist. The transfer of power to the management, inherent in the process of industrialisation, has in a sense been reversed. Again, making individual specialisation superior in terms of influence compared to the task-specialisation dominating the first part of the industry society.

A collapsing triangle?

In this chapter, we have discussed society as socially constructed in the sense that scholars such as Berger & Luckmann (op. cit.) and Weick (op. cit.) analysed reality and organizing respectively, combining it with the theorizing of Watzlawick (op. cit.) and Allport (op. cit.). All of them suggesting societies to be "exteriors", or "atmospheres", filled with everlasting interpersonal communication.

Not everything, however, in a society is concerned with work and people working. Many other practices have been socially constructed as well as elaborated constituting a bigger picture – our realities – surrounding the MC-triangle. Communication as a structuring mechanism has, though, an outreach far beyond that of work and related activities. As Watzlawick claims, "you cannot not communicate". Supported by McLuhan's "the media is the message" (1964). Reality talks to us! And we talk back.

In this chapter work and communication are discussed primarily related to the work of professionals. Actually – in professional settings – work and communication collapse into being two sides of the very same coin. Two perspectives that are mutually defining as well as expressing each other, or, putting it differently – among professionals, work equals communication, to allude to the world's most famous equation.[9]

Having said that, the question remains concerning what to do with the management corner of the triangle. Work back on top, merged with communication due to the nature of knowledge work, collapse the triangle to one relation and one relation only. Between work and communication on the one hand and management on the other.

Analysing the MC-triangle from the point of view of social constructionism also makes management, of course, socially constructed. The worldview, as used here, thus implies an observer as well as an observed something.[10] Reality literally emerging in-between observers and observed. And, therefore, playing out in the social interconnectedness of interpersonal communication. Communication, though, is the relational substance creating the social space in which we live.

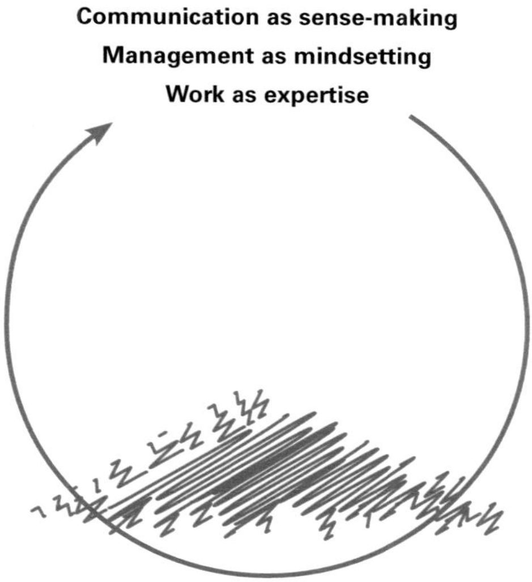

Figure 5. A complete circle and merged processes collapsing the triangle.

The recognizing aspect of social constructions makes for example managerial leadership subject of being something admitted. A manager might be viewed as superior or inferior as leader which influences the dynamics among that manager and others and his or her co-workers. Good leadership, though, is an opinion and, utterly, what people perceive watching a person. Do they see a leader or not? Do they recognise leadership in what a person does or say? The answer will of course vary and yet, shared values and opinions tend to promote a dominating opinion. At least when people talk about somebody and calibrates, as well as modifies, their opinions. The expression "you are appointed manager but have to earn your leadership" illustrates well our position on this subject.

For these reasons, management, and for that matter leadership as well, might be viewed as absorbed into communication when the MC-model is applied on knowledge work. Leadership, though, becomes a question of people's values and judgements and their attribution of meaning to reality. Putting all parts of the MC-triangle at the very top in the case of specialists and knowledge workers provides a single point in a sphere of (otherwise socially constructing) ongoing communication. A kind of shared power and influence between managers and knowledge workers eliminating the hierarchical features of organisations, or better; making superiority a matter of circumstances and thus a constantly shifting aspect within a given social setting.

Accepting the claims in this chapter, though, is putting communication at the very top of the MC-triangle. After traveling a complete circle of the corners around it. From the down right-hand side of communicating – that is craftsmen and craftswomen talking about and organizing their assignments – passing the left-hand corner and communication as organisational flows of information – and lastly, becoming the structuring mechanism of reality. Including the components of the initial MC-triangle simply by absorbing them, making MC only three aspects of the same social process.

It seems, though, as if the MC-triangle survived both crafted and industrially manufactured products but did not make it through a socially constructed society of knowledge work and specialist services. Having the knowledge workers and specialists regaining power concerning approaches to creating values at the expense of those having managerial duties and ditto positions. At least relatively speaking. Perhaps all might be summarised as if a collapsing triangle simultaneously closed a circle.[11]

Notes

9 We use the word "allude" to alert the reader to the fact that our expression is not mathematically correct. Due to the fact that all human activity is not work as work is defined here. But substituting work with energy-usage also makes the reversed expression true. Since every human activity consumes energy. And work and energy have a lot in common. Especially in the field of physics. We may claim that energy-usage (activity) equals communication – and vice versa! As Watzlawick puts it – "you cannot not communicate".

10 With self-awareness as an interesting special case of observer/observed relations.

11 Although, reminding the reader that the MC-triangle may still be useful for analysing a lot of other kinds of work situations as well as jobs besides those being the focus in this particular chapter.

References

Allport, G. (1954). *The nature of prejudice.* Reading, Mass: Addison-Wesley.

Argyris, C. & Schön, D. (1978). *Organizational Learning: A Theory of Actions Perspective.* Reading. Mass.: Addison-Wesley.

Berger, P. & Luckmann, T. (1966). *The Social Construction of Reality.* London: Penguin Books.

Berle, A. & Means, G. (1932). *The modern corporation and private property.* New York: Macmillan.

Csikszentmihalyi, M. (1990). *Flow: The Psychology of Optimal Experience.* New York: Harper and Row.

Drucker, P. (1959). *Landmarks of tomorrow.* New York: Harper.

Duyvendak, J., Knijn, T. & Kremer, M. (2005). *Policy, People, and the New Professional. De-professionalisation and Re-professionalisation in Care and Welfare.* Amsterdam: Amsterdam University Press.

Kuhn, T. (1962). *The Structure of Scientific Revolutions.* Chicago: University of Chicago Press.

McLuhan, M. (1964). *Understanding Media: Extensions of Man.* London: Routledge.

Morgan, G. (1986). *Images of Organizations.* Thousand Oaks, Calif. SAGE Publications.

Pfeffer, J. (1981). *Power in Organizations.* Marshfield. Mass.: Pitman Books.

Schein, E. (1985). *Organizational Leadership and Culture.* San Francisco: Jossey-Bass.

Schwab, K. (2016). *The fourth industrial revolution.* New York: Crown Business.

Watzlawick, P., Beavin Baveals, J. & Jackson, D. (1967). *Pragmatics of human communication: a study of interactional patterns, pathologies, and paradoxes.* New York: Norton & Co, Inc.

Weick, K. (1969). *The social psychology of organizing.* Reading, Mass.: Addison-Wesley

Werr, A. & Furusten, S. (Eds) (2016). *The Organization of the Expert Society.* Abingdon: Routledge.

CHAPTER 6

Managing time and time-horizons

Abstract

In this chapter, management, strategy and planning is put in the centre, from the perspective of time. Time (and timing) is fundamental for all forms of organizing and management, as well as strategic improvisation as the mindset argued for in this book. Regardless of the work patterns among individual managers, plans have been a dominating approach to coordinate actions and activities towards predefined objectives. Time was an aspect of production, of course, in Taylor's time-motion-studies and also in contemporary concepts such as just-in-time, time-to-market and time management. In the chapter earlier studies on organisations and management are described – long-range planning, strategic management, visionary leadership – as well as quarterly capitalism.

TIME IS A CENTRAL PART of contemporary managerial thinking and a fundamental dimension of strategic improvisation, which we will demonstrate later. Historically, governance and leadership has been associated primarily with territories (Machiavelli 1532, Heilbroner 1962). From its very earliest modern versions, though, management has been occupied with time (Tyrstrup 2005)[12] and increasingly so. Time was an aspect of production, of course, in Taylor's time-motion-studies. However, also in contemporary concepts such as just-in-time, time-to-market and time management. The latter, being a hype during the 1980s, until managers realised that managing their time management calendars consumed more of their time than was saved by the approach. Below we briefly portray the significance of time, and in particular time perspectives, as determinants of different approaches to management and a fundament of strategic improvisation. The claim is straightforward. A continuously shortened time perspective reflects the eroding efficiency of a main tool for management – the plan and, thus, planning as a method for guiding activities in organisations!

The gateways of managerial leadership

Since Taylor, among others, sketched out the basics of modern management, primarily activities such as designing organisations, planning operations and making decisions – all in advance – the direction of managerial influence was assumed to be obvious. Putting it differently, what executives and other managers managed was the future and what should happen there! This was the expectation among employees as well as managers and still usually are. An expectation, though, violated when Sune Carlson, professor of management at Stockholm School of Economics and later Uppsala university, raised the question "What do executives do?" and decided to answer it empirically (Carlson 1951). Carlson's main finding, even more valid today, was that executives do not control their agendas. Rather, the executives in Carlson's study, dealt with things that had already happened but, for some reason, needed their attention. Carlson revealed a pattern of pronounced reactivity in managerial work and behaviours, the very opposite of the expected future orientation of executive leadership. Carlson's findings were repeatedly confirmed by prominent scholars such as Henry Mintzberg (1973) and Rosemary Stewart (1976) studying a variety of managerial positions. The studies by Carlson and Mintzberg were replicated during the last decade of the 20th century by Tengblad (2000), a professor of Human Resource Management. Tengblad confirmed that executives react to circumstances rather than shape them. A difference, though, was that Tengblad noticed that executives spend a significant proportion of their time with business journalists and financial analysts, change Tengblad attributed to the increased interest in shareholding.

The reactive pattern in managers work bothers them of course although they are aware of it from their everyday experiences. In management education, as an example, managers often talk about their desire to be less involved in everyday issues and rather attend to strategic matters instead. Duties they must worry about during weekends, in the cab on their way to the airport, or in the kitchen preparing the family's dinner. Today, Carlson's findings are so well established that this kind of studies are not done anymore. Focus is rather on the various expressions as well as symbolics of managerial leadership (Alvesson & Sveningsson 2003) and the organisational processes managers are involved in (e.g., Holmberg & Tyrstrup 2010).

Tyrstrup, one of the authors of this book, suggested that the relevance of managerial leadership was not to be found in what was planned but rather in what was not planned (Tyrstrup 2005). A manager makes his or her contribution to effectiveness and efficiency by dealing with the unexpected, typically, exceptions in need of their attention. This is done by an improvising leadership approach (Tyrstrup 2006). This put managers in a work mode of almost constant sense-making to facilitate actions here and now and to nurture long-term development of people's mindsets within as well as around the organisation. This cultivation is done primarily by interpersonal communication concerned with interpretations of what is happening. Including the guidance inherent in sketching out a set of possible implications. Back, though, to the expected future orientation of managerial leadership but in a very different way than formal planning and consistent with a reacting or improvising approach to managing organised operations.

Co-workers as well as other stakeholders of an operation understand what is offered and done in that very operation in a particular way. It may concern car production, rocket science or crime investigation, all grasped as activities providing some kind of value and doing so to someone identifiable. It may be a consumer, a citizen or a business partner, yet, an understanding of a business that is neither randomly shaped nor rock solid in its constitutions. Rather, it is an outcome of earlier sense-making and present in the constant process of ongoing interpretations.

A changed mindset changes what is recognised as being offered, how and to whom. These changes may take place instantly. As when the app-based smartphone, being a computer the size of a palm, replaced the traditional cell phone. The latter being limited to making phone calls, texting and listening to voice mails, the former being the interface to the world.

It was very clever of Apple to call their version iPhone, keeping attention on it as a phone rather than the key to people's digital life. That is, the rearranged and even merged business-models of a former phone industry and the contemporary internet industry. More often, mindset changes through small steps nudging behaviours in a certain direction (Thaler & Sunstein 2008). As when vinyl records were replaced by tapes, then moving on to CDs and further to the current streaming using smartphones and headsets. Innovations such as these rearrange roles such as consumers and suppliers but also business models, value chains, and logistics, making us all content providers of a constantly evolving digital universe. This is a historical journey – in both senses of the word – possible to feature as changed time perspective and successively reformed approaches to management.

Long range planning

Regardless of the work patterns among individual managers, plans have been a dominating approach to coordinate actions and activities towards predefined objectives. Or, more precisely, doing so at the organisational level rather than the individual (Hales 1993), making applied time perspectives the determinant of what is regarded as feasible and efficient. Especially the urgency of matters and the horizons of what is known or can be considered as reasonably certain. So, let us start at the very peak of management as scheduling. That is, the application of long-range plans or planning (LRP) to manage actions during the mid-20th century.

Roughly speaking, LRP were about making regular budgets, however with a time perspective of ten years or, in some cases, even longer than that. There are examples covering a time horizon of fifteen years. This does not mean, however, that budgets were done every tenth year and only then. Budgets were successively replaced, thereby modifying the LRP, at a pace of every two to four years or so depending on the stability of the environment a business operated in. The circumstances, and the pace by which they were changed, did modify the budgeting processes and, thus, the outcomes in terms of updated versions of the LRP.

A ten-year time perspective was motivated by the fact that the industries, at that time, were investment intensive, and therefore, almost by definition, required a distant time horizon. Comparing individual budgets over time exposes fine tunings that adjust the LRP to changes within the companies as well as its environments. In fact, investing in real-capital – plants, machines, tools, vehicles, office buildings – is congruent with the LRP approach to management. Important to emphasise is that long-range planning occurred during an era when precisely doing that – planning many years ahead – made sense. They were not stupid people! It was very different times. Yes, the pace of development in most areas was also high and intense then. The direction, however, was well known and to a certain degree therefore predictable. This was, as an example, the time when President Kennedy challenged the United States to put a man on the moon before the end of the 1960s. And, as some might recall, not because it was easy but precisely the opposite – because it was hard. It was the era of mighty projects such as building larger and larger oil tankers and developing the first and thrilling versions of computers used in the Apollo missions. It was the era of spectacular as well as long-ranging plans – in business and in politics – aiming at transforming society. Not always because it was hard. Rather because it was possible!

Strategic management

At the same time as the Apollo project, H. Igor Ansoff, a Russian-born and later American physicist and mathematician, made a drastic career move. First, he became a scholar and consultant as opposed to his earlier career as manager in large technical corporations. Second, he changed the line of expertise from physics and mathematics to management science. Ansoff was among those who articulated a growing doubt in working with LRP. And he launched an alternative – based on the concept of strategy[13] (Ansoff 1965) and strategic management (Ansoff 1979), a concept developed not only by Ansoff himself but many others at the time.[14]

In 1973, the oil crises surfaced. The oil-producing countries, collaborating within OPEC, decided to reduce global production by several percentages thereby creating a price building process on the brink of chaos. Most of the developed countries suffered heavily, having large parts of their energy systems based on oil. Programs were launched to reduce the use of electricity as well as ration the access to oil and its different derivatives. The latter, not least aiming at reducing the private use of gasoline and diesel. However, the global economy was transformed in other areas as well. New countries, such as Japan and South Korea, entered the global stage of manufacturing. Large parts of European production were relocated to Asia. This, of course, created massive domestic problems in terms of unemployment and industry crisis deeply structural in nature. Rarely has the world economy transformed so rapidly as well as radically in just a couple of decades.

The conclusion was obvious. The world was no longer developing in accordance with either earlier patterns or recognisable pathways. Regions around the world, as well as countries, experienced structural changes which altered people's lives rapidly. Local areas could find themselves in deep crisis while others prospered as never before. Complete sectors collapsed! Such as the textile industry and the shipyards in Sweden. Others, such as media and telecoms could not find enough educated people to support their expansions, domestically as well as internationally. The keyword at the time was flexibility and its counterpart – in terms of looking ahead – was strategy.

Strategies can be seen as a kind of "rule of thumb" for how organisations should act to develop their businesses. Within, though, a time frame of five to perhaps seven years. Examples of strategies are companies growing by acquisitions as opposed to organically. Another example was to offer existing customers new products and services. Or, of course, the opposite. Offering existing products and services to new customers. Also aiming at dominating different markets through growth and size was a popular strategy. As well as the very opposite, targeting niches or segments with less intense competition or no competition at all. Anyhow, summarised and more generally though, strategies are ways of acting with potential to create, or fulfil, a set of strategic advantages within the up-coming years, restricted by the kind of organisation that it concerns. Public organisations often had strategies such as improved employer branding, increased service quality and higher effectiveness by competence development. A lot of public employees were occupied with implementing what was called New Public Management (Ferlie et al. 1996). Non-profit organisations recruited sponsors among people shopping at weekends instead of calling them on their phones at home (Ciconte & Jacob 2009). This is mentioned just to give a flavour of strategies other than those applied in commercial enterprises, and a reminder that other kinds of organisations tend to imitate for-profit businesses.

It is often assumed that the private sector, being subject to the pressure of competition, represents the premium form of rational and innovative ways of managing undertakings. The concept of new public management, shaped during the era of Thatcherism and Reaganomics, did precisely that – encouraging the public sector to imitate the private. Although the very core of Margaret Thatcher's and Ronald Reagan's policies was to reduce the very size of the public sector making the whole economy more efficient and not only the public services within a strategy of replacing public undertakings with private and, thus, presumably more efficient solutions. It was, in fact, an era of large-scale privatisation. Not only importing private business management to the public sector.

Ansoff referred the need for strategies primarily to difficulties in detailed planning and the lack of proper preconditions for precisely doing that. Another scholar, Drucker, however, noticed a more fundamental transformation of both the kinds of values that were created as well as how. He claimed that two major, but related changes were unfolding. First, the change within Western economies moving from manufacturing products towards providing services. Second, a corresponding change, in the kind of needed expertise and relevant know-how or skills. The transformation towards more of knowledge work – in a world of emerging discontinuities – would also require more of a qualitative approach to managing organisations (Drucker 1969) as opposed to the earlier more quantitatively oriented. Strategies could be expressed in qualitative terms and, in fact, were preferably formulated that way. Long-range planning, on the other hand, relied more on quantifying the representations of reality and its development trajectories.

In the late 1980s and early 1990s, strategies and strategic leadership were found to have their own limitations and shortcomings however, without making them obsolete. They were still good – but not good enough. Strategies informed people about in what ways an organisation should be developed as well as how to accomplish that. However, one important question remained unanswered – why? Strategic goals only informed employees, in hindsight, if a goal had been accomplished or not without any urgency or importance attached to the particular outcome – thus, the qualitative benefits of a success and ditto downsides in case of a failure.

As already mentioned, strategies are not obsolete; however, they are apparently not sufficient for organizing and managing the value creation in post-industrial organisations. This is reflected in a growing interest in the cognitive as well as socio-cognitive aspects of human collaboration, adding visions to the toolbox of leadership approaches.

Visionary leadership

To fully grasp the emergence of visionary leadership, we must understand how the role of employees changed in the decades before the turn of the millennium. Thus, having left the 1970s with its conspicuous health issues among employees, well-being of humans becomes a pronounced issue in both leadership and in particular human resource management. This is also when administration of personnel is transformed into precisely managing human resources.

Extensive routinisation in the 1950s and 1960s created a working life with too much unhealthy monotony. Especially in manufacturing but also in some clerical work. It is, therefore, no coincidence that concepts such as purpose and meaning became fundamental in the discourse on leadership during the last decades of the 20th century (e.g. Smircich & Morgan 1982), including ideas on self-managing teams (e.g. Hicks & Bone 1991) and empowerment of, but also trust in, employees (e.g. Sims & Manz 1996). At that time people were recognised as engaged in sense-making and, in fact, this being crucial for their health. A view turned into a model of humans in much theorizing in contemporary social sciences at the time.

Shifting perspective from within organisations to looking at them from outside reveals a significance of what was called corporate image or ditto reputation (Gray & Balmer 1998), defined simply, what comes to people's minds and their associations when noticing a particular organisation. New research concluded that these thoughts and images have implications for people's readiness to use its products or services as well as their attitudes towards working for the organisation. An important feature of an external perspective is recognizing the behaviours of organisations and the ethics that can be attributed to these behaviours. Good citizenship was regarded as strategic (Jones 1980), making corporate citizenship a central theme concerned with successes and failures (Graham 1995). People's opinions were defined as well as refined in sense-making and communication processes, which may promote or destroy organisations. This is part of the background to why visions became the new mantra (Bennis & Nanus 1985). Highly skilled and educated knowledge workers did not become specialists to simply make a living or accomplish some figures suggested by the advisors of an executive team. Their know-how was available and offered only to organisations appreciating true professionalism and striving for some meaningful purpose. Profits – of course – to be able to pay the salaries they deserved, but also bringing new things to the world, being the best, doing important stuff, making a difference, all within an air of excellence – the expressions varied of course. It most certainly heralded personal brands and being head-hunted.

Knowledge workers expect to be consulted about what the organisation should do, as well as how and why! Anchored in their professionalism, they regarded themselves equally competent as the management to sketch out the road maps to success. Leadership was supposed to provide the preconditions for professional achievements and, therefore, also the prosperity of the organisation. Professionals and specialists wanted to be invited to the processes in which the paths to the future were formulated and their claim was simple: If the leadership provided a vision – as the cognitive infrastructure and coordinating mechanism of the mission – they would contribute with the service content necessary to excellence.

Thus, leaders and leadership were put at the very forefront of securing organisational prosperity. Visions, in the shape of exciting illustrations of a future to come, would provide the necessary understandings of what to accomplish and especially why. The visions were occasionally complemented with a mission statement featuring in a sense how people as well as the society would benefit from the realisation of the mission. In that way, visions and missions made up the kind of mental sphere and motivational atmosphere promoting ideas to flourish and innovative thinking to take off. In that sense, co-workers were invited to be part of an intense and engaging undertaking into a successful future. Within, let us say a timespan of three years or so. Visions do not necessarily have to be bounded in time. However, as mentioned and to the extent they are, the typical time perspective is a few years, and, shorter than its predecessors for overall business leadership and organisational development. Alternatively, they are, for a particular reason, defined in terms of an upcoming year. A celebration, a year with a significance of its own, or so far into the future that it lacks relevance and just communicates a diffuse "forever".

The concept of visions rhymes better with the awakening interest in employees' competence, motivation, and importance as contributors to value creation and organisational success. This was mirrored in a leadership fostering transformation (Bass 1990), a concept usually discussed in contrast to its alternative – the transactional approach to leadership. The latter being about exchanges rather than changes, particularly in terms of incentives for contributing to value creation. Transforming, however, focus on meaning and purpose of an undertaking. As mentioned at the beginning of this book, narrative approaches have been around for some time (but have a renaissance now). Already in the 1980s concepts such as storytelling and creating narratives found their way into management theory and practices (Weick & Browning 1986) and became included in the many recipes for successful leadership.

To summarise, a vision is an engaging image of what people, as a collective, wanted to be or become. And therefore also, collectively, want to stand for or represent. An identity-formation and a mutually constructed meaning concerned with the wider importance of a business or the case of the public sector, valuable services provided to citizens. In general, though, answering the question why do we exist as an organisation? What do we bring to the world? These are the kind of rather demanding claims that were made when the importance of visions should be illustrated.

Quarterly capitalism

In her campaign for presidency of the United States, in 2016, the democratic candidate Hillary Clinton concluded in a statement.

> “ I am deeply distressed about quarterly capitalism because I think it is causing businesses to make decisions that are not helping the long-term profitability of American corporations or the success of our economy.[15]
>
> HILLARY CLINTON, 2016

Within a period of slightly more than half a century, the time horizons – especially in larger and listed companies – were reduced from 15 years to 15 weeks. At least metaphorically speaking and perhaps not quite that dramatic. But, certainly, from a decade or so, to one or at most a few years ahead with a pronounced attention on here and now. To quote the well-known American best-selling author Joseph Heller – “Something happened” (1974).

There are, of course, exceptions in that some references to issues in the future go far beyond a few years. Sometimes even further than decades, for example, an announced date when it will be illegal to drive cars running on fossil fuels or the expected lifetime of a new highway. But such examples put aside, the time horizon in management and leadership has been steadily shortened over the last decades.

Quarterly capitalism is a negatively charged expression. Those acting within a long-term perspective, it is often claimed, as by Hillary Clinton, embrace not only different but better values than those taking impromptu actions. At least that is how we usually think when we discuss time perspectives in leadership. Framed as a question of choice – as something that can be chosen in a non-trivial sense. Other analytical options, like the one we embrace, open for those who perceive a VUCA-like world around us. Short-term actions are, perhaps, a rational approach to the characteristics of a complex and unpredictable society. It could even be argued that the transformation from long range planning (LRP) to today's short-term perspective, precisely reflects the evolution of a VUCA world. The question is therefore not why executives choose to act in a short-term manner. The question rather becomes whether we have reached the end of traditional management based on planning and as the quantitatively typical governance model within society, irrespective of sectors.

Regardless of the exact answer to such questions, we must consider a fundamental issue. If circumstantial conditions make short-term actions rational, what then would a suitable governance approach look like? At a group level, as mentioned, it can be claimed that a joint improvising approach is reasonable (Tyrstrup 2006). But at an organisational level – including frequent inter-organisational collaborations – what are the options here? When the preconditions for applying traditional management are not met very well!

David Weinberger, American philosopher, argues in his book *Everyday Chaos* (Weinberger 2019), that knowledge is in a state of alteration. From being fixed in its constitution and hierarchically structured it has become more fluid and networked. Knowing is not as important as the ability to associate. The Internet, Weinberger continues, has democratised access to both information and know-how for better and for worse. Blueprints for making nuclear as well as chemical weapons are for instance available on-line and this truly challenges rigid distributions of knowledge as well as what can be kept secret. Putting us, Weinberger claims, in a mode of constant change – yes, declared for decades – but more intense in contemporary societies. Thus, making adaptability a crucial collective response capability and joint sense-making the very essence of making decisions in a turbulent world. People, though, are encouraged to rapidly agree on what is going on and act accordingly. Usually by improvising the Carpe Diem version of life in the expert societies of the VUCA world.

After telling the story of what and why – focusing on the historical and contemporary changes in the work-management-communication triangle, and the transformation of leadership and management – we now enter the world of how. In the following chapter we tell the story of strategic improvisation, aiming to show how this idea and paradox mindset may be the answer to all the questions and challenges that we now stand in front of.

Notes

[12] Today space is highly relevant to management although as strategies, for example internationalisation, or locations, such as building plants and offices or systems for logistics and transportations.

[13] A concept borrowed from the military world as with so many other words in management. For example, line-staff organisation, divisions, tactics and so on, and so forth.

[14] The concept of strategic management evolved in the 1950s and 1960s with contributions from primarily Peter Drucker, Philip Selznick, Alfred Chandler, Bruce Henderson and, as mentioned, H. Igor Ansoff.

[15] https://www.businessinsider.com/hillary-clinton-quarterly-capitalism-2016-4?r=US&IR=T

References

Alvesson, M. & Sveningsson, S. (2003). *Managers Doing Leadership: The Extra-Ordinarization of the Mundane.* Human Relations, Vol. 56, Iss. 12. pp. 1435–59.

Ansoff, H.I. (1965). *Corporate Strategy.* New York: McGraw-Hill.

Ansoff, H.I. (1979). *Strategic management.* London: Macmillan.

Bass, B. M. (1990). *From Transactional to Transformational Leadership: Learning to Share the Vision.* Organizational Dynamics, Vol. 18, Iss. 1, pp. 19–32.

Bennis, W. & Nanus, B. (1985). *Leaders: The Strategies for Taking Charge.* New York: Harper & Row.

Carlson, S. (1951). *Executive behaviour: a study of the workload and the working methods of managing directors.* Stockholm: Strömberg.

Ciconte, B., & Jacob, J. (2009). *Fundraising Basics: A Complete Guide.* Burlington, Mass.: Jones & Bartlett Learning.

Drucker, P. (1969). *The age of discontinuity: guidelines to our changing society.* New York: Harper & Row.

Ferlie, E., Ashburner, L., Fitzgerald, L. & Pettigrew, A. (1996). *The new public management in action.* Oxford: Oxford University Press.

Graham, J. (1995). *Leadership, Moral Development, and Citizenship Behavior.* Business Ethics Quarterly, Vol. 5, Iss. 1, pp. 43–54.

Gray, E. & Balmer, J. (1998). *Managing Corporate Image and Corporate Reputation.* Long Range Planning, Vol. 31, Iss. 5. pp. 649–802.

Hales, C. (1993). *Managing through organisation: management process, forms of organization and the work of managers.* Abingdon: Routledge.

Heilbroner, R. (1962). *The making of economic society.* Englewood Cliffs, N.J.: Prentice-Hall.

Heller, J. (1974). *Something happened.* London: Cape.

Hicks, R. & Bone, D. (1991). *Self-managing teams.* London: Kogan Page.

Holmberg, I. & Tyrstrup, M. (2010). *Well Then – What Now? An everyday approach to managerial leadership.* Leadership, Vol. 6, Iss. 4, pp. 353–72.

Jones, T. (1980). *Corporate Social Responsibility Revisited, Redefined.* California Management Review. Vol. 22, Iss. 3. pp. 59–67.

Machiavelli, N. (1532). *De Principatibus.* Rome: Antonio Blado d'Asola.

Mintzberg, H. (1973). *The Nature of Managerial Work.* New York: Harper & Row.

Sims, H. & Manz, C. (1996). *Company of heroes: unleashing the power of self-leadership.* New York: Wiley.

Smircich, L., & Morgan, G. (1982). *Leadership: The management of meaning.* Journal of Applied Behavioral Science, Vol. 18, Iss. 3, pp. 257–73.

Stewart, R. (1976). *Contrasts in management: a study of different types of managers' jobs: their demands and choices.* London: McGraw-Hill.

Tengblad, S. (2000). *Executive Behaviour revisited: perspectives on a classic work within management research.* Gothenburg: Gothenburg Research Institute.

Thaler, R. & Sunstein, C. (2008). *Nudge: improving decisions about health, wealth, and happiness.* New Haven: Yale University Press.

Tyrstrup, M. (2005). *Sovereigns of time – A Scandinavian view of executive work, time, and leadership.* Lund: Studentlitteratur.

Tyrstrup, M. (2006). *On the brink of failure – The art of impromptu action in everyday Leadership.* Lund: Studentlitteratur.

Weick, K. & Browning, L. (1986). *Argument and Narration in Organizational Communication.* Journal of Management, Vol. 12, Iss. 2.

Weinberger, D. (2019). *Everyday Chaos. Technology, Complexity, and How Were Thriving in a New World of Possibility.* Boston, Mass.: Harvard Business Review Press.

CHAPTER 7

Strategic improvisation – the art of balancing order and chaos

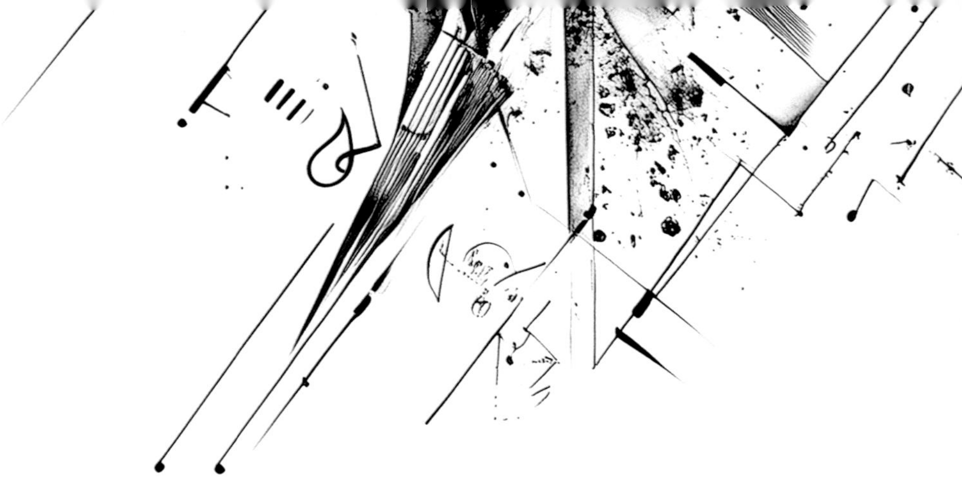

Abstract

This chapter takes the stand in the need of a late modern leadership in the VUCA world, based in a historical understanding of organisations and management. In the chapter the concept and model of strategic improvisation is presented and discussed. The aim of strategic improvisation is to enable us to navigate both order and chaos, perform the balancing act between complexity and the ever-changing nature of everything, and to establish a clear direction. Ultimately, strategic improvisation fulfils the basic needs for stability, security, and shared values. The model for strategic improvisation consists of three supporting parts: strategy, narrative, and improvisation. It should not be interpreted as a linear process but where the different parts continuously fertilise each other. Strategic improvisation means a narrative adapted to the situation within a given framework. Strategic improvisation occurs when three essential components are combined: a clear strategy (the framework), professional interpretation and making of purpose (the narrative), and situational adaptation based on given opportunities and conditions.

STRATEGIC IMPROVISATION IS the intersection of two seemingly contradictory logics. As previously described, being strategic involves meticulous planning and wise, well-balanced choices based on rational decisions. In contrast, improvisation embraces creativity, letting go, and acting intuitively. Thus, strategic improvisation includes both order and chaos, with the addition of narrative logic. However, in practice, these concepts are not at odds; instead, they are prerequisites for one another. As we will illustrate, they mutually reinforce each other and are vital for effectively navigating the intricate demands of the VUCA world that today's organisations and leaders face.

To be relevant and credible, as well as to consider an ever-larger sphere of stakeholders and an increasingly complex surrounding world, both leadership and an organisation that promote employee commitment, creativity, and situational adaptation are required. Simply put, more strategic improvisation is needed. This leadership philosophy becomes particularly important for those who aspire to be societal actors, who want to contribute to something bigger, who have the drive and will to think innovatively and act in alignment with their time and surroundings.

When the map does not match the terrain

As we discussed in previous chapters, modern organisations operate under the strong belief that both people and organisations are rational entities. The foundational assumption is that management efforts can be planned and executed and can achieve pre-set goals. Consequently, planning and formulating goals becomes a crucial task, followed by evaluating whether these goals have been achieved. The organisational approach is linear: an organisation plans and engages with its selected stakeholders according to a predetermined order. Organisations are perceived as stable, bounded, and sensible systems capable of communicating from the inside out in a controlled manner. Aligned with the modern and rational thought model, researchers have developed models and theories that explain which method applies across various contexts.

The tacit knowledge

But when researchers get closer to what happens in practice, confusion arises. The reality in practice does not appear to be particularly planned, and the simple connections between plan and effect are difficult to find. The disordered practice is full of random events, changing conditions, and unique situations. We can state that, parallel to the belief in the ordered worldview, there is a large amount of tacit knowledge among leaders, which is translated into practical action that can be difficult to describe in words. Tacit knowledge (also called hidden, implicit, or unspoken) is experience-based, practical, and created through extensive practice. Some aspects of it are highly individual, while others are universal. The commonality lies in the principles, methods, and approaches used to manage the constant stream of order and chaos, creating balance and progress in a complex context. This tacit knowledge serves as the starting point for our model of strategic improvisation, and in the next chapter we illustrate how it is expressed through principles, methods, approaches, and organisation.

That the map does not match the terrain is not a new insight but has been rediscovered in various areas over many years. The fact is that in one of the first descriptions of strategy by Sun Tzu in the *Art of War* (5th century BC), flexibility and adaptation to situation and context were emphasised in a rather developed way. In modern times, many researchers – not least within organisational theory – have questioned the rational and linear view of organisation, including the previously mentioned organisational psychologist Karl E. Weick, who completely questioned the rational view of organisations as well as the belief in linear control and information dissemination. Another example is Herbert Simon, who received the Nobel Prize in Economic Sciences in 1978 for his research from the 1950s on decision-making that showed people's bounded rationality. A concept that illustrates that people in decision-making situations start off from the prevailing situation, rather than from a perfect information basis. In a decision-making situation, people do not manage to take in all conceivable information, nor formulate all conceivable decision alternatives. Instead, they absorb certain information and rely on their previous experiences. Outwardly, however, they try to hide this afterwards and describe their decisions as being made on a completely rational basis. A similar line of reasoning is advanced by the Swedish organisational theorist Nils Brunsson. In his questioning of the sanity of organisations and decision-makers, he states somewhat simplistically that the only thing organisations do is imitate each other through loads of meaningless reforms, strategies, and policies. There are heaps of other organisational researchers who similarly marvel at the strong belief in rational and linear management models.

The need to be adept at improvising based on ever-changing conditions is also well-known in crisis management research. This is for the simple reason that crises in themselves are so unpredictable that it is rarely possible to plan for their course or consequences. While the perceived uncertainty, changeability, and speed characterise the environment in which contemporary organisations operate, at the same time it is increasingly difficult to distinguish normality from a state of crisis – that is, decisive events with serious consequences.

The strategic improvisation model

We need tools, methods, and approaches for late modern leadership in the VUCA world. These will enable us to navigate both order and chaos, perform the balancing act between complexity and the ever-changing nature of everything, and establish a clear direction. Ultimately, they help fulfil our basic needs for stability, security, and shared values.

The model for strategic improvisation consists of three supporting parts: strategy, narrative, and improvisation. It should not be interpreted as a linear process but where the different parts continuously fertilise each other. We are sceptical of a simple twofold division of strategy and implementation because such a division is based on linear thinking where "a" gives "b" which gives "c". Rather, our starting point is that different applications of the strategy, and their effects and consequences, will continually change and develop the strategy – as in a circular motion.

Strategic improvisation thus means a narrative adapted to the situation within a given framework. Whether it involves processes carried out over many years or operational decisions made at the minute, the pattern remains the same. Strategic improvisation occurs when three essential components are combined: a clear strategy (the framework), professional interpretation and making of purpose (the narrative), and situational adaptation based on given opportunities and conditions.

We have taken the idea of strategic improvisation from several areas such as the creative-artistic sector, some research in management and strategy (e.g. Moss Kanter 2002, Marren 2008, Pina e Cunha et al. 2012, Tyrstrup 2007) and crisis management. The latter is not so surprising, given how crucial it is to act rapidly based on an uncertain decision basis during emergency events (Falkheimer & Heide 2022). Or as the boxer Mike Tyson supposedly said, "Everybody has a plan until they get punched in the mouth."

However, our main inspiration comes from music, which we believe has both words, theories, and experiences of high relevance for leaders in all types of organisations. Music teacher Arne Forsén at the Royal Academy of Music in Stockholm described what improvisation is in the world of music. His input gave us the foundations of our model, parts of which we present below. The experiences of recent years from the pandemic, climate crisis and war in Europe have also contributed to the development of the model. Here, the importance of stories and narratives has again become very clear.

THE STRATEGIC IMPROVISATION MODEL

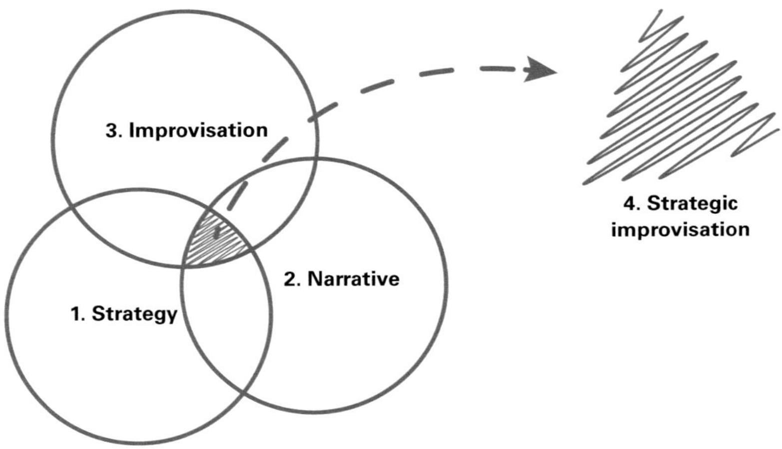

Figure 6. Strategic improvisation occurs when strategy, narrative and improvisation are combined.

1. Strategy (or composition)

In the world of music, the composition is the piece of music to be performed as planned – the choice of key, time signature and dynamics, length, instruments and more. Also known as the notes. In an organisation, this can easily be translated into the documents that will guide the direction and structure of the business. For a company, this can be business plans, visions, and goals. For an authority an operational plan, regulation letter. In a region or a municipality, the political budget is an important governing document. It can also include more comprehensive strategy documents – multi-year plans, brand platforms – as well as laws or other regulations that the business must comply with. Strategy is there as a necessary structure and is the basis of the business. It provides guidelines and indicative priorities to start from.

To effectively manage a business and demonstrate good leadership, one needs knowledge of rules and an understanding of the business's conditions, logic, and strategies. This knowledge and understanding become particularly crucial when making decisions and choosing directions, not least as a motive for priorities and decisions made. Except for rules or laws set outside the organisation, the importance of strategies in an organisation is determined largely by how the strategy is developed and maintained. For the strategies to have any actual effect on the business, the employees must have been involved in their development and formulation. Involvement and communication are required both before, during, and after a strategy process. Otherwise, there is a risk that the documents will merely become shelf warmers. In that sense, the process is often more important than the documents themselves. Additionally, as mentioned, strategies must be agile and continue to adapt to changing conditions.

Some organisations get stuck in the industrial logic we described earlier, allocating significant resources to strategy development and planning, so much so it sometimes hampers operations. Conversely, other organisations allocate minimal time and resources to frameworks, potentially compromising strategic governance and the overall stability of the business.

Our experience is that moderation is best. The importance of comprehensible, manageable, and meaningful governing documents should not be underestimated; creativity and situational adaptation cannot take place in a vacuum. You can compare it to a jazz orchestra – a comparison we will return to – where a clear basic beat is needed to hold the music together and make the musicians confident enough to improvise. The basic beat should sit in the spine and be a given landing place after the soloists' excursions, which never happens beyond the overall idea. Strategy (or composition) is sometimes perceived as the opposite of improvisation. However, this is a gross simplification. Composed music does not always have to be sheet music and remember that musical improvisation is often based on rehearsed, imitated, and repeated formulas. This fits well with our model of strategic improvisation – as something that requires not only flexibility and freedom but also a clear structure from which to start. Without a framework, it is actually very difficult to improvise, and not very safe.

2. Narrative (or interpretation)

Interpretation is a concept in music that involves the musician's interpretation of the author's intention and composition. The musician asks him- or herself about the choice of tempo, phrasing, dynamics and much more. What does the composer want to convey with the composition? What feeling should be evoked? Through the musician's experience, competence, and creativity, the interpretation is the result that makes the material his or her own. If all musicians interpreted the composition the same, the result would be identical. Which, of course, never happens.

In the daily activities of an organisation, an interpretation is continuously made of what one wants to achieve and what is required to get there. The interpretation is simply the questions that leaders and employees constantly struggle with in their everyday lives when trying to apply different solutions to their problems and challenges, for example: How can we contribute to the business reaching its goals? How can we connect what we are going to do to the overall organisational strategy and business plan?

This interpretation is expressed in narratives of various kinds and a leader's ability to craft a compelling narrative is crucial for strategic improvisation within an organisation. Without a firm belief in the organisation's purpose and a shared *raison d'être,* employees lack the courage and direction needed to fully improvise strategically. Why do we exist? How do we want to be and act? You can take this a step further. To find a purpose beyond mere performance, we must, as mentioned in an earlier chapter, invest time and energy in forging a common interpretation and purpose – the common narrative. What do we want to contribute to society? How do we act honestly and credibly? Conducting the discussion about the narrative in work teams and at employee gatherings, in everyday meetings and at annual kick-offs is a crucial ability and task in late modern leadership. The shared narrative allows employees to interpret their own roles and assignments. How do I contribute to the business? What space do I have to act within? In what ways does my work affect the whole?

Narratives exist at every level because they are a form of communication, deeply ingrained whether acknowledged or not. Consider Ukraine's strategic narrative in its fight for its nation and global democracy – a narrative aimed at both its citizens and the Western world at large. Another example is in the United States, where two parallel narratives underpin the worldviews of Republicans and Democrats.

3. Improvisation (or situational and mutual adjustment)

For a musician, improvisation means reusing older material, putting it together with something new and thereby configuring it in a new way in front of a certain audience and in a certain environment. Improvisation therefore has to do with flexibility, creativity, and innovation. But at the same time, the process is not completely random: there is a thought, a plan, a rhythm to rest against. In the same way, improvisation works outside the world of music: the party leader must connect to the party's ideological values, the company leader to the business plan, the director general to the authority's instruction and the municipality's officials to the politicians' decisions.

As mentioned earlier, musicians who improvise usually start from a certain basic beat, some kind of predetermined form. This provides a secure base that allows for relaxed and free improvisation. It is the basic beat that sets the framework for the improvisation. If the organisation wants to be an active societal actor, it must also operate and act in harmony with its surrounding society. It requires continuous and intensive listening about what issues people want to discuss, what needs have arisen and what opportunities or counteracting social currents have appeared. If you want to take a broad social responsibility, you must be in dialogue with your surroundings and have a high ability to change. Without a genuine interest in the surrounding society and a high inner desire for change, it is impossible.

When composing, there is the opportunity for reflection and correction, but in an improvisation, all choices must be made in the moment. Improvisation works in the same way in management and leadership. When a strategy and narrative are well-established, the discovery of an internal or external event enables swift improvisation. The action can be here and now, in this minute, but can also be changes in the much longer term. This can be described as the ability to pivot your strategy or engage in incremental strategy development. To constantly have the skills and courage to adapt and experiment, reuse, and develop your strategy is essential because not everything can be predicted.

4. Strategic improvisation

Improvisation requires boundaries to be meaningful. In music, this delineation involves choosing musical material and forms; in theatre it refers to a story to be told, casting and planning events. An overabundance of ideas or rapid transitions between ideas can make the overall picture incoherent and dull. In strategic improvisation, the framework and narrative provide these necessary boundaries to move freely within. The improvisation is not random and aimless; there is a clear direction in the impulses that are chosen to act on and the opportunities that are exploited. It's not about being a rebel that pushes the boundaries, but rather being one who innovates within them. Understanding what fits within the established framework and narrative and leveraging them to their fullest potential.

Strategic improvisation thus occurs when these three components are combined: a clear strategy (the framework), a professional interpretation (the narrative), and situational adaptation based on given opportunities and conditions. By applying strategic improvisation in concrete leadership and co-workership, organisations increase their chances of becoming successful and relevant social actors. All the components must be in place at every level: in the foundational starting points for the business, in the organisation, culture, and leadership, as well as within everyone. Leaders and employees must possess the ability and prerequisites to strategically improvise in any situation and have the tools and knowledge to effectively carry out this type of late modern leadership. Furthermore, the organisational structure and work processes must align to create the conditions necessary for this way of working.

Before we take a closer look in the last chapter at how strategic improvisation is concretely applied based on three leadership principles, we will see what some researchers have said about improvisation.

The six elements of strategic improvisation

Rosabeth Moss Kanter (2002) at Harvard Business School has studied how quickly established companies connected their operations to the Internet, as it emerged. One conclusion was that the companies that were late to the ball and thereby also reduced their competitiveness had three traits in common. First, they were closed systems, sceptical of new ideas. Second, there was a reluctance to open and listen to employees' ideas. And three, these organisations were top-managed and always awaited the decisions of top management. When these organisations eventually realised that they had to keep up with the developments, the development efforts often ended up alongside the regular operations. Those who developed positively in relation to the new technology tended to act before they had a clear plan, encouraged innovators in the organisation to test solutions and projects, quickly adapted to customers' changing needs and usage, and connected everything with regular operations. Through an open and encouraging climate, employee engagement was created:

> They did not wait to act until they had a perfectly conceived plan; instead, they created the plan by acting. In short: they improvised.
>
> MOSS KANTER 2002, P. 76

Kanter believes that traditional strategy can be compared to traditional theatre where scripts and planning are the focus. The actors practice their roles by repeating their script until they know everything by heart. Everything should be predictable. In contrast, she highlights improvisational theatre, which is then also linked to innovation:

Pina e Cunha, Clegg and Kamoche (2012) believe that the focus will then be on how organisations should secure their own position rather than disrupting the balance through innovative and entrepreneurial efforts and changes. In other words, a consequence of the traditional strategy and competitive thinking is that organisations become conservative and repeat themselves, rather than renew themselves. Porter's model and other similar models adopt a macro perspective, while a cognition and improvisation perspective rather starts from what happens on the floor of the organisation and includes faster changes:

> (...) the view from the operations room can be remarkably different from the one that obtains at the top: it changes swiftly, reveals unexpected opportunities and threats, and requires more than purely analytical skills.
>
> PINA E CUNHA, CLEGG AND KAMOCHE 2012, P. 266

They further believe that the ability to constantly listen to one's surroundings, interpret signals and implement changes on an uncertain basis has become increasingly important. One reason for this is the enormous flow of information that we live in. Acting roles within the organisation should function as explorers, closely connected to everything that is happening. Opportunities are discovered through active participation on the ground, rather than by sitting and observing the world from a control tower. This mindset has been established for quite some time and has been formulated in words and concepts such as "blue ocean strategy", "agile" or "radical innovation" and sometimes, but not as often, as improvisation, the concept we think is the most relevant. Of course, strategic improvisation shares similarities with an agile or innovative mindset. But also stands out, partly because we begin from a basic sense-making communication perspective on organisations and adopt ideas and theories originating in the creative and artistic sector, particularly the world of music.

Pina e Cunha, Clegg and Kamoche (2012) also highlight the importance of improvisation. They define organisational improvisation as "the conception of action as it is unfolding and drawing on available resources" (p. 268). They believe that the improvisational mindset has not had any major impact on the strategy area. Inspiration has rarely been drawn from the artistic realm, but rather from traditional strategy. According to them, the fundamental reason for this is the Western world's view of the world, where explanation and planning dominate over acting in the moment. You can compare this to how we humans are shaped in a culture where we equate information with communication – where there are only senders and receivers and no room for interpretations and complexity. Strategy, according to the dominant plan model, is similarly a matter for top management, who then anchor, but above all, market the ideas to everyone else. Strategy as improvisation is a continuous process that is fundamentally collective: planning and action happen simultaneously, different voices are heard, and the actual strategy document is in constant change.

Seven jazz principles for increasing organisations' improvisational ability

Professor Frank J. Barrett is the organisational and leadership researcher who most prominently highlights the importance of embracing jazz improvisation in organisations, within the research world. In addition to emphasizing this in several scientific articles, he published a magnum opus, also aimed at professional practitioners, with the appropriate title *Yes to the mess* (Barrett 2012). His connection to this thinking is not so surprising given that, alongside his research, he is a well-qualified jazz musician.

Barrett believes that leaders must adopt a mindset that maximises learning, embraces opportunities that arise in the moment, and simultaneously strengthens long-term, dynamic organisational capabilities. Like the other referenced researchers, and in the reasoning about the importance of time, dynamic ability is considered decisive for counteracting organisational stagnation. His and his colleagues' approach to jazz improvisation is based on the same basic assumption – acting quickly here and now, but within a clear framework – that we pursue in this book:

> Jazz improvisation is a prototype of an organisation that builds up routines and yet also values novelty and emergence – an approach that resonates with dynamic capabilities research.
>
> Bernstein & Barrett 2011, p. 60

Mainly based on qualitative research in the form of observations, Barrett has synthesised his ideas into seven principles:

1. ALL THAT JAZZ: Mastering the Art of Unlearning: This means that it is important to create renewal so that employees do not just repeat the same thing over and over. Otherwise, the risk is stagnation and that employees get stuck in established routines that create no value and above all no innovations. Skilled jazz musicians venture into uncharted waters from time to time by challenging prevailing structures. For this to succeed, courageous leaders and employees who dare to question the established are required.

2. YES TO THE MESS: Developing Affirmative Competence: Improvising jazz musicians must compose in the moment with limited control and ability to predict where one is going. A situation that can easily be translated into how leaders are forced to act in changing organisations in a changing world. One way to deal with these situations is to alternate between looking back, trying something new and seeing how it works:

> The musician therefore looks back on what is emerging – the various chord progressions, melodic fragments, rhythmic patterns – and then jumps into the morass, seeing the potential for embellishing on motifs, linking familiar with new utterances, and adjusting to unanticipated musical cues that reframe previous material.
>
> Barrett 2012, p. 69

3. PERFORMING AND EXPERIMENTING SIMULTANEOUSLY: Embracing Errors as a Source of Learning: This principle is based on the importance of creating a safe and learning organisational culture. When employees are allowed to participate, express themselves and try things out, their commitment also increases. This also means that as a leader you must allow mistakes and dare to let go of control.

4. MINIMAL STRUCTURES AND MAXIMUM AUTONOMY: Traditional organisations are often overburdened with control and governance structures through rules, documentation requirements, target management and so on. While many of these structures are necessary and stipulated by legislation, many can be dismantled, as they are neither necessary nor add any value other than management feeling that they control more than they de facto do. Structure and framework are needed, but organisations must also create opportunities for employees to be creative and innovative. This is most effective in loose systems, particularly within smaller creative groups where different skills cross-fertilise each other – much like in a jazz band.

5. JAMMING AND HANGING OUT: Learning by Doing and Talking: Organisations must create room for both random and planned meetings and conversations. This is often when new ideas and methods are developed. Informal forms of meetings plus time and space to talk, learn from each other and develop new solutions correspond to the jam sessions when musicians create something new.

6. TAKING TURNS SOLOING AND SUPPORTING: Followership as a Noble Calling: In jazz, rotating leadership during performances is well established. It is not just a single leader who is at the centre of attention; all musicians take their turn in the spotlight. The formal leader then assumes a withdrawn role and, together with fellow players, supports the musician currently in the centre. This same leadership mindset is needed in organisations, according to Barrett.

7. LEADERSHIP AS PROVOCATIVE COMPETENCE: Nurturing Double Vision: This principle serves the same purpose as the first, to relearn and learn new things. However, here the leader's role is emphasised in this process. The starting point is as a leader, you perceive that your work group's potential and opportunities are not being fully utilised. This necessitates changes that turn existing practices upside down. While such insinuations may create enthusiasm for some and irritation for others, without provocations, perhaps nothing will happen at all. Barrett highlights Miles Davis and Duke Ellington as prominent figures within "provocative competence".

References

Barrett, F. J. (2012). *Yes to the Mess: Surprising Leadership Lessons from Jazz.* Boston, MA: Harvard Business Review Press.

Bernstein, E., & Barrett, F. (2011). *Strategic Change and the Jazz Mindset: Exploring Practices that Enhance Dynamic Capabilities for Organizational Improvisation.* Research in Organizational Change and Development, Vol. 19, pp. 55–90.

Falkheimer, J. & Heide, M. (2022). *Crisis Communication as Strategic Improvisation.* In W. T. Coombs & Sherry Holladay, Eds. The Handbook of Crisis Communication. 2nd ed. Malden, MA: Wiley-Blackwell.

Marren, P. (2008). *Strategic Improvisation.* Journal of Business Strategy. Vol. 29 No. 6, pp. 59–61.

Moss Kanter, R. (2002). *Strategy as Improvisational Theatre.* MIT Sloan Management Review, Winter 2002, Vol. 43, Iss 2, pp. 76–81.

Pina e Cunha, M., Clegg S.R., Kamoche, K. (2012). *Improvisation as "real time foresight",* Futures: the journal of policy, planning and future studies, Vol. 44, Iss. 3, pp. 265–72.

Tyrstrup, M. (2007). *Organisatoriska mellanrum – om kompetens, samverkan och godtycke i kunskapsintensiva verksamheter. (In translation: Organizational in-betweens – on competence, collaboration and arbitrariness in knowledge intense undertakings).* Centre for Advanced Studies in Leadership, Research Report Series, No 12.

STORY

Keith Jarrett and the Köln concert

THE BEST-SELLING IMPROVISATIONAL JAZZ RECORD of all time is believed to be *the Köln Concert* by Keith Jarrett. This incredible piece of music has inspired many and made numerous memories. The concert is a live recording from a midnight concert on a winter night in 1975.

For us, the Köln concert is an excellent example of strategic improvisation: a situational interpretation within a given framework, performed in a now.

The world should be very grateful that the concert was recorded that very night. When questioning whether it could be replicated, the answer is, of course, no. We should actually be thankful that the concert took place at all.

The concert was intended to be a midnight performance at the Cologne Opera House, part of Keith Jarrett's 1973–74 European tour featuring solo concerts of improvised music. The conditions in Cologne were dismal. Keith Jarrett was unrested, had travelled extensively, and was reluctant to perform. The grand piano to be used was in poor condition with some non-functional keys. Being a Friday night meant that finding a replacement grand piano, one that could be transported in the drizzling rain without falling out of tune, was impossible.

Keith Jarrett decided to cancel, but the 17-year-old organiser, Vera Brandes, ultimately persuaded him to perform. They called in a piano tuner who, within five hours, managed to get the grand piano into a playable condition–at least sufficiently.

With these conditions, world-class music was then created. A single concert that since has been played millions of times. What made this so outstanding? Was it the framework, the limitations, the specific situation? The "now'?

Keith Jarrett's producer Manfred Eicher has speculated that the fact that the grand piano was in such poor condition may have contributed to the quality of the concert, by forcing Keith Jarrett to exert himself to get sound out of the instrument.

It is also speculated that strong and emotional memories of Cologne, perhaps from a love story years earlier, may have inspired Keith Jarrett's performance.

What we do know is that the music created that night has since sold a total of 3.5 million records. And that it made improvisation history.

CHAPTER 8

Strategic improvisation and narratives in applied management and leadership

Abstract

In this final chapter narratives and strategic improvisation are applied in concrete management and leadership. Three fundamental management principles are defined, described and exemplified. The foundation for this is all the research mentioned in the book, many years of practical experience in communication, management, and leadership, as well as several conversations and interviews with successful managers. The three fundamental management principles are a well-planned framework (strategy), a responsive ability to act (improvisation) and a clear and common narrative. The three principles concretise the application of strategic improvisation, where one is about re-creating preparedness for uncertainty and constant change, and the other two about creating direction, context, and shared meaning.

IN THE PREVIOUS CHAPTERS, we have been able to state that more of a modern leadership and new forms of organisation are required to succeed in the VUCA world, where meaning-making and the ability to balance order and chaos are so crucial. Our starting point is that we are in a time where, according to our previously presented triangle model consisting of work, management and communication, the latter is placed at the very top. In this triangle, human work has evolved from craft to designed jobs, and then to knowledge work & services, management has evolved from stewardship (direct leadership) to management (indirect leadership) followed by interpreting the leadership, and communication has evolved from talking to information, followed by narrative sense-making. Based on all the research we have mentioned, many years of practical experience in communication, management, and leadership, as well as several conversations and interviews with successful managers in earlier work (Falkheimer & Gentzel Sandberg 2017, 2019), we can state that strategic improvisation in practice is based on three fundamental management principles:

1. Well-planned framework
2. Responsive ability to act
3. Clear and common narrative

The three principles concretise the application of strategic improvisation, where one is about re-creating preparedness for uncertainty and constant change, and the other two about creating direction, context, and shared meaning. Now we will illustrate how the principles express themselves in organisation and approaches in leadership. The description that follows can be summed up in the following matrix:

	STRATEGY	IMPROVISATION	NARRATIVE
PRINCIPLE	A well-planned foundational structure	Responsive action capability	Powerful images and stories
ORGANISATION	Focus on value creation, predictable and robust Room for innovation, development, and flexibility	Rigged for constant change Iterative processes and learning loops Room for manoeuvre	Co-production with employees and other stakeholders
APPROACHES	Connects the short and long term Provides predictability Reminds of the vision and what creates value Equips the organisation	Makes functional and intuitive decisions instead of optimal ones Sees failure as natural and necessary Cultivates a culture of trust and takes responsibility for mistakes	Explains, repeats and reminds Talks the walk Walks the talk Is present and accessible

Table 1: Matrix of Fundamental Management Principles.

Leadership principle 1: *A well-planned foundational structure*

The business strategy, long-term planning, vision, regulatory letters, laws, ethical agreements, and the owner's directives are examples of documents and stated ambitions that form the framework within which we all must operate. In some organisations, this framework provides stable support for work and serves as a reliable backbone for decision-making. However, others may find the framework too vague or unclear. For a third group, the framework can be too restrictive, even suffocating and potentially stifling critical thinking. In such cases, doing things right becomes more important than doing the right things.

Focus on value creation, predictable and robust

In a changing social context, the organisation needs to act flexibly and improvise strategically. However, this is not possible without a functioning framework that provides lasting stability and direction. The governing documents provide direction for the business and steer towards the value-creating core processes, regardless of the complex shifts in the outside world. Within creative professions and other contexts where improvisation is common, people often talk about the importance of defining limits because it is a way of getting structure. With a clear basic structure, it is often easier to be creative. If you don't know what you are allowed to do and where you are going, you also don't know which path to take. As illustrated in *Alice in Wonderland*, when Alice asks which way to go, the cat's obvious answer is: "That depends a good deal on where you want to get to". But answering that question is not always so simple.

The challenges with a well-planned basic structure are perhaps most evident in start-up companies. A start-up company, by definition, has no history to fall back on and must run quickly to be able to create an offer. The horizon is extremely short. The possible planning time is maybe a year, anything further is insurmountable. A vision can lie with a time horizon as short as three years away and planning often takes place quarterly.

In recent years, it has become clear that the rest of society must also relate to the faster conditions and logic, in the same way as a start-up. Just think of the pandemic and the recession cycles that arose during that period: from disaster to recovery to cost crisis again. This places new demands on both organisation and approach and keeping the strategy tight enough. The need for focus and direction will perhaps become even more important, but at the same time must take place with a shorter horizon.

While these concepts might not be novel, they have gained renewed importance due to the added pressure and accelerated pace of change of the outside world.

Room for innovation, development, and flexibility

Contemporary innovation researchers have found a dilemma once suggested by James March (1991) – that organisations must focus on either innovation (exploration) or efficiency (exploitation) – to be passable. Steiber & Alänge (2013), for example, based on a study at Google, claims that a certain corporate culture, combined with a semi-structured organisation and an empowering leadership, allow constant improvement and ditto innovation to coexist. They suggest some modifications of efficiency work to better comply with an innovative environment. They talk about a set of organisational characteristics for continuous innovation as the recipe for coming to terms with March's dilemma. Here, there is both a structured production organisation and room for innovation, and these principles operate in parallel.

Different people with varying focuses coexist within a common framework. With respect for each other's different roles and behavioural profiles, something unique is created. Innovation work has been integrated into the core business to generate synergies through small or large steps. Leadership plays a crucial role in making this work; it requires managers who can create order and security while also stimulating employees and creating conditions for renewal. A higher purpose is needed – an answer to "why" – with leadership that drives the culture, where much of the work is based on self-organisation.

Connects the short and long term

In the VUCA world, there is a risk that managers might become too engrossed in day-to-day business. Therefore, the ability to set a clear direction becomes crucial and reminds everyone of what creates value, which in turn establishes stability and a foundational structure for the employees. Every individual needs to be prepared for our societal context to be in constant flux, while also being reminded of what is predictable and robust.

The manager needs to stay one step ahead, focusing on core processes and value creation. They should lift their gaze and remind everyone of the long-term vision and "why". A management task involves maintaining balance and connecting short-term goals for the week or quarter with the long-term vision. It's essential to recognise that unforeseeable events will occur, and the organisation will need to address them, but not necessarily how these shall be addressed. While it's impossible to create an approach for every situation, shared goals among employees and a narrative extending beyond the immediate assignment allow for adaptable structures to be put in place quickly.

Provides predictability

The simplest foundational structures and core processes provide the basics for being able to improvise. It is important to remind employees of how things are usually done and what the routines are when everything is as usual. Almost all new situations can be adapted to an approach that is already in use; entirely new routines are rarely necessary. It is simply a matter of finding similarities with something else. In a crisis, it is crucial to make a fairly quick transition from being entirely reactive to creating predictability and resilience, as people cannot endure unpredictability for too long. Those who successfully identify constants perform better as managers.

Reminds of the vision and what creates value

There is a balance between control and freedom. Foundational structures and frameworks naturally differ across organisations, but there is much that unites in how leadership must function. Managers who are to help people improvise must create a clear structure, highlight what is constant and the direction, remind of the vision, and help sort out what creates value. The manager's task is to assist employees in focusing on the task at hand. To feel supported and safe, knowing that the manager stands behind them.

People can only improvise when they perceive a degree of freedom. Different professions have varying views on their ability to influence work and act freely. Those who sense no freedom to act can very easily become passive or dissatisfied. Managers face the often-tough challenge of convincing everyone that there are always opportunities to make an impact, even if they may be limited. All must have room for creativity, despite any perceived constraints.

Equips the organisation

A State Secretary in a former Swedish government once shared that in difficult situations and when making tough decisions, they prepared by "putting on armour". Dressing in armour is a way to give the wearer a bit more courage, power, and strength, so-called power dressing. Actors can also emphasise the importance of costumes in fully immersing themselves in their roles. Another form of attire is the uniform, which transforms the individual into a professional, imbuing them with a sense of security, experience, and calm.

In everyday life, we encounter lab coats and police uniforms, for instance, which can evoke this type of impact and sense of authority. A social services manager described how they always carry a reflective vest in their bag. It has come in handy on several occasions – not because they walk around waiting for disasters, but because it's good to be prepared when something happens. In their professional role, one can suddenly find oneself in situations where it's beneficial to present oneself and create a sense of security. The reflective vest signals some form of order, structure, and control in a chaotic situation. It signals "I am someone to turn to".

The uniform or suit doesn't necessarily need to be visible. You have heard of the expression "to get into character" which means to go inward, embrace one's personality, and dare to stand up for something. When fundamental values are shaken, they mobilise and become exceptionally clear within themselves and who they are. It's crucial to stand up for what one believes in, both as a manager and as a human being.

Leadership principle 2: *Responsive action capability*

The second leadership principle is based on the view that there is never a completely constant starting point and that there are always uncertainties that cannot be planned for. Order and chaos exist side by side. A successful societal actor realises that we live in a complex and unpredictable VUCA world in constant change, where the significance of time, as previously discussed, is crucial. Therefore, the ability to improvise, to act responsively depending on new situations and conditions, will always be necessary.

Rigged for constant change

A fundamental prerequisite for strategic improvisation is this precise insight: that there is always uncertainty and that there will always be events and situations that cannot be predicted, the so-called X factor. The only thing one knows for sure is that it is impossible to know exactly what will happen. This requires – as described in the first leadership principle about a well-planned basic structure – demands on sustainability and robustness to adapt to changes in the long term and continue to develop. The basic structure of the organisation should remain fixed, but equally important is to organise for great flexibility for the unexpected and unplanned. The processes and structures are in support of what is crucial for success: constant adaptation and improvisation.

This is being rigged for constant change. A result is that it becomes non-prestigious to change one's mind or to make mistakes. When people have succeeded in embracing uncertainty in various ways, it becomes something challenging and exciting instead of something that disturbs ingrained routines and ways of working.

Iterative processes and learning loops

The starting principle of the changeability of everything has consequences for which core methods one uses to build their organisation and leadership, how one prioritises, and the choices one makes. It is evident how different the reasoning becomes when leadership and organisation stem more from flexibility and an agile mindset than from planning and control.

Strategic improvisers base their leadership on the attitude that leadership is about adapting and adjusting to what changes. If constant change is instead the norm, as a societal actor, one aims to operate as well as possible amidst this ongoing flux with ever-evolving conditions. The key lies in swiftly recognizing effective methods within the specific context and promptly assessing when it is time to change.

Perhaps this is most evident in the start-up culture: adaptive operations where the development curve is anything but linear. Where there is no history, and new problems requiring new solutions arise every day. This means that the percentage of failures is greater than in older organisations. However, it also becomes evident that if there are no failures, there is no development. This is solved by working in rapid iterations and learning loops – feedback and evaluation that result in direct adjustment and development. Often, the business is broken down into very small units. Agile iterations and scrum are common working methods in the start-up sector. Because the more each activity is broken down, the faster development can occur: This week, "this" should be done to reach "this" month's goal. With such a short horizon, it is not a disaster if that week's activity is a fiasco, since it is just a small unit that has failed. There seems to be a greater acceptance of failure in a start-up because there is a greater inherent understanding that success is not a linear process. You build success by learning from mistakes and by testing your way forward. With the organisation in such small iterations, it is easy to fail, because it is just about a week's loss. A three-year plan that collapses on the other hand, is something completely different.

Room for manoeuvre

Today, time is scarce. Events proceed whether the organisation keeps up or not. Changes and development happen quickly, and an organisation that stands still and waits is moving backwards. It's about creating a manoeuvring space, a lead, so that you're ahead of events instead of chasing after them. Professionals in emergency services are trained to quickly become operational and often have to make decisions based on poor and incomplete information. This makes professional intuition crucial. There is much to learn from those with extensive experience in making decisions on incomplete information: the police, the midwife, the social worker, or the start-up entrepreneur. Here, decisions often involve creating room to manoeuvre to control events, instead of chasing after and trying to correct what has already happened. The reasoning is that it is almost always better to decide and act in some way than not to act at all. In administrative organisations, it can be the complete opposite; the best thing may be to do nothing at all, and it will work out anyway. But in a VUCA world, there is much to learn from the approach of operational activities: doing nothing at all can have devastating consequences. Taking the initiative is crucial to steer the course of events.

Makes functional and intuitive decisions instead of optimal ones

Being a leader during uncertain conditions requires something different than in the traditional sense where the boss is expected to be meticulous, and things may take their time. Here, quick decisions on uncertain grounds are required, which means taking greater risks.

The idea of making functional decisions based on limited information emerged in organisational research decades ago but has probably never been as relevant as it is today. Many probably wonder: are we playing a strategic chess game or an intuitive game of chance?

In certain professions, this is such a fundamental prerequisite that it becomes ingrained in employees' DNA. Within emergency services and the military, employees are trained from day one to act amidst constant uncertainty and change as if it were the norm. Already as a foot-patrolling police officer, one learns to make decisions under stress based on insufficient information, and then adapt as the situation evolves. Leadership is based on quick decisions that are functional here and now, even if their long-term effectiveness remains uncertain. Managing emergency services often involves continually filtering out poor decisions rather than seeking the optimal ones. However, functional decision-making is crucial even in the manufacturing industry. Company management testifies to an exponential curve, often reaching 80 percent certainty in decision-making swiftly. However, striving for 90–95 percent certainty can be futile as circumstances may have already changed. In even the slowest manufacturing processes, a manager must make decisions here and now, with the clarification that while an immediate decision is necessary, new information may soon surface that could necessitate adjustments.

Sees failure as natural and necessary

In fast-paced situations, there's a high risk of making mistakes and things going wrong. At the same time, failures are necessary to develop. Without failure and the courage to risk failure, there is no learning and no success. When failures occur, the relationship with one's own manager becomes particularly clear. Leadership becomes a matter of getting employees to see the value in daring and the importance of being willing to fail. Showing understanding and acceptance, that failures can teach us something, and that one always lands softly.

In police operations, there is extensive experience with this. As a manager, one must be aware that mistakes will occur during operational situations. It is easy to see in hindsight how things should have been done, but in the moment, it's very challenging. Everyone does their best based on the existing conditions at that time. Mistakes can happen, and they must be allowed to happen, but we must learn from them. The crucial aspect is purpose ethics. If the purpose and intention are to do what is right, then one should not be penalised if mistakes occur.

Recruiting individuals with a "start-up mentality" who have a pragmatic view of what constitutes failure, is a preference within start-up circles. Employees who don't fit into that environment often become stressed by the perception that it is chaotic, "nothing works", and that there is no plan. To function effectively, everyone must take their own initiative, knowing that mistakes can happen, yet recognizing the value of initiative regardless of the outcome. It's better to try and fail than to do nothing at all. When mistakes occur, they serve as valuable lessons for future endeavours. Doing nothing leads to neither accomplishments nor learning. There is a genuine perspective that failure presents an opportunity for improvement and serves as a learning experience. One can normalise failures through a straightforward narrative and infuse it with other connotations. One example of such a strategic narrative is "mistake scars", which employees who have faced setbacks carry with a sense of pride. This suffering also contributes to success and status. Others shift perspectives and realise that organisations fail too infrequently. Here, the argument is that without failures, one remains too much in a safe place and doesn't learn enough.

When people fail, leadership is most important. A manager takes responsibility for what went wrong in private, and in such moments, all available support must be in place. There's no need to delve too deeply into the specifics of what happened. Rather than punishing, providing hindsight, or blaming, the focus should be on acceptance – these things happen when operating in a complex world. Demonstrate that we are together, and our collective focus is on finding solutions. This strengthens the group.

Cultivates a culture of trust and takes responsibility for mistakes

If there is no understanding of failures, insecurity quickly sets in – the first sign of a lack of trust. Therefore, "What do you think?" should be a common phrase in the management of the VUCA world. Decisions and resolutions should be delegated to those who are closer to the challenge and often have better decision-making information than the manager who is furthest from the challenge. Every employee should have a clear responsibility and assignment and have reasonable conditions in terms of resources and mandate. Mandate means that the manager truly does not interfere with how employees choose to solve their assignment but trusts that each employee can decide what is best.

People must also be able to trust each other as a group. The improvising actor must trust that their scene partner enters at exactly the right moment, and a musician cannot play a solo indefinitely. What has been agreed upon must hold. In the scouting movement, everyone is trained to take responsibility and always trust in everyone's abilities, even the seven-year-old. The reason it works is that each person has been given a moderately challenging task, even if they are only seven years old. Scouts reason that you don't have to like each other, but you do need to trust each other. People may argue and disagree, but we trust that we are doing our best and that we help each other.

In cultures of trust, there is an understanding that many processes are beyond our control. There are opposing forces with their own will, irrational approaches, missing knowledge, and things that simply happen. This mindset is crucial. No matter how well we have prepared and planned, things can still go wrong. But mistakes mustn't be due to carelessness or nonchalance. Sometimes things turn out well because of luck, and other times they go poorly due to unfortunate circumstances. Phenomenal efforts can lead to terrible outcomes, while mediocre efforts – with some luck – can yield fantastic results. The role of a forerunner is crucial in creating such a culture. It's essential to foster an environment where no one is perfect, not even the boss.

Even in the most extreme situations, when significant values for an entire country are at stake, a culture of trust is a successful strategy. Researchers Ekman & Nilsson (2022) have shown that Ukraine, for example, during the first year of the Russian invasion, have operated based on what they call a one-voice policy. This approach involves fundamental narratives that should be spread, with a conviction that the communication is effective, simple, and clear. The country's leadership has realised that using bureaucratic language from government agencies is not effective for conveying messages that the population needs to act upon. Instead, they assign tasks to civil society organisations and private communication agencies, knowing that these entities have a much better ability to rapidly spread communication. Always with the underlying message: we can win this!

Leadership principle 3: *Powerful images and narrative*

We have observed that a well-planned foundational structure is necessary. Hopefully, it provides stable support in a context of constant change. However, the rigid framework needs to be complemented with a softer management approach that creates meaning by demonstrating vision, direction, and employees' motivations. Earlier in the book, we also noted that what drives societal development and growth, and what motivates people to achieve great feats, is not numbers but narratives or stories. Narratives unite groups and inspire them to achieve feats far beyond expectations and hopes. Narratives involve mental structures that establish a culture and perspective, and leadership ability plays a fundamental role in this context.

Managers must therefore create genuine meaning in their organisations and among their employees – which can also include customers, users, suppliers – by rallying around the answer to the question of why. Why the organisation exists, what is its unique contribution to the outside world and society.

The opportunities for strategic improvisation are facilitated with a common narrative that everyone can agree on. And strategic improvisation facilitates a sense of coherence. Managers who realise the importance of helping their employees and their organisation to a sense of coherence and social benefit will also create good conditions for strategic improvisation. Because when employees feel secure, they dare to improvise. There is agreement on where one stands today, what it means, and what choices need to be made, both big and small.

The furniture company IKEA represents several well-known and highly vivid narratives. Many of them stem from the document "A Furniture Dealer's Testament" that the founder Ingvar Kamprad once formulated. This document, today called "the IKEA way", clearly shows that IKEA is not built on rules but on values, and this makes a significant difference for leadership. The content helps both managers and employees with which values apply, the core of IKEA, but also with the direction forward and how everyone can contribute to this.

An estate developer in a completely different industry shared an instructive story about the importance of everyone seeing themselves in a larger context and how they contribute meaningfully (Falkheimer & Gentzel Sandberg 2019):

> " I was given responsibility for an excessively large construction project when I was just 20 years old. I was ambitious and tried to optimise resources so that we could manage with 23 excavators instead of 25. But at the slightest disruption, the construction came to a halt for two days, following a classic queue system, and no one understood why. After the holidays, I thought, "Let's do the opposite". We broke everything down into smaller units of around 25 people, each managing themselves, being autonomous, and solving problems over coffee. We got such a positive development of the

project that I still can't quite grasp what happened. The first year went poorly, and the client was dissatisfied with our delivery. However, in the three years following the change, we made money, had fun, and the client was satisfied. The tactic that made all the difference was grouping the massive project into smaller manageable and meaningful units. That experience left such a strong impression on me that it has influenced everything I've done since. It's so crucial that the mission is comprehensible for everyone, and decisions should be as close to the individuals as possible. If you try to remove this "bottom-up" force, you're pulling the rug out from under them. You can beg for ownership and engagement, but if there is too much that the employees don't understand or can influence, it won't work.

FALKHEIMER & GENTZEL SANDBERG 2019, P. 106

Co-production with employees and other stakeholders

This fact is equally relevant at both the organisational and national levels. As this book is being written, the world awaits the outcome of the 2024 US presidential election. Just like in many other elections, the narrative about the nation takes centre stage. In another part of the world, in Ukraine's struggle in the war against Russia, it has been noted that the war is not only won on the battlefield but also in the minds of people, in an ongoing battle over what is true. Ukraine's communication strategy is based on a central narrative that can be communicated in different ways, depending on the context, target group, and goals. *We can win and we will win, but we need help as we are not only fighting for Ukraine but for the survival of democracy worldwide.*

Ukraine has set up its national communication apparatus based on informal networks that can mobilise very quickly. It is not just the established bureaucratic structure that manages the country's narrative, but tasks are assigned with quite free hands to various actors around the country, such as civil society organisations, independent editorial offices, and private communication agencies. Researchers (Ekman & Nilsson 2022) state that there is professional respect and insight that sometimes there is a greater opportunity to reach out with the overall narrative if others mediate it than the state. At the same time, there are antagonistic narratives created by other forces. The ambition is for them to be perceived as true, to be picked up in the West, and ultimately to turn the world in another direction. Against the Western world or any other chosen country. Or at least they intend to weaken the support and thereby the democracy.

Explains, repeats and reminds

Having a shared narrative is crucial for creating meaning, understanding the mission and recognizing one's role within it. However, the process of establishing this shared understanding is not as straightforward. Our experience is that it is usually not specific moments or a particular action that has resulted in a good outcome. Perhaps the key is something as simple as an ongoing conversation?

The method for achieving shared ownership is to assist employees with what the assignment is and in what societal context the organisation operates. With the help of narratives, the manager assists employees in interpreting the surrounding society, their roles and assignments, and the culture and context of the organisation – constantly, year in and year out – a narrative is kept alive.

Talks the walk

Another way is to create new minor narratives using words and concepts that describe what needs to be done and how. It's about "talk your walk". A term like "mistake scars" in the start-up world, as described earlier in this chapter, is a clear example of how, using loaded words, we want to normalise failures. Another example is "ship it!" Get the product out there! There's always room for better code or design, but the products must go out in start-ups. Time is limited, and knowledge of the market isn't extensive enough. It's only when the product meets the market that learning occurs. "Ship it" is an example of instilling in employees that the company's products don't always need to be better than "good enough".

In non-profit organisations, understanding one's own narrative is crucial. These discussions about narratives can be both numerous and lengthy. Perhaps it's inherent in the very fabric of the non-profit world that there exist as many interpretations of the organisation's mission as there are engaged individuals? Clearly, managers in the non-profit sector must invest significant time and effort in crafting a shared story that defines the organisation's identity and direction – a story that everyone can contribute to and build upon.

Walks the talk

Narratives are also expressed through words and actions – "walk the talk". People's behaviours have a greater impact than one might think, and as a manager, this must be made conscious and explicit. A social services manager recounts an instance when she was tasked with setting up a crisis support centre with just a few hours' notice after a terrorist attack. The centre would be staffed by employees from various organisations who had never met before. Each day began with a mandatory half-hour briefing, emphasizing the centre's purpose, the tasks of the staff, and the collective goal of providing calm, security, and care. As a manager, she also had to lead by example: moving slowly, speaking softly. During the first hour each day, this manager would walk around and remind the staff: what signals do you send if you rush, speak quickly, and raise your voice?

Is present and accessible

Being accessible is almost always identified as the most crucial skill for managers who adhere to the principles we describe. Personal presence needs to exist in everyday conversations, regular meetings, and even at the coffee machine. Here, the manager picks up on moods and emotions. It's not always physical availability that matters, but rather the importance of conveying the feeling that one can be reached at any time. Being present rather than merely available. It's akin to the sense of having an insurance company – you don't necessarily need to make contact, but it feels reassuring to know they're there.

This reflection is also evident at the national level, as seen in the example of Ukraine. In hindsight, it was understood that the international community expected the Ukrainian government to evacuate itself. However, that didn't happen. Instead, a plan was put in place for leadership communication through daily speeches, clear messages, and recurring narratives. A present leadership that remained in Kyiv, communicating endurance, hope, and resilience.

References

Ekman, I. & Nilsson, P-E. (2022). *Ukraine's Information Front – Strategic Communication during Russia's Full-Scale Invasion of Ukraine.* Report FOI-R--5451–SE. Totalförsvarets Forskningsinstitut.

Falkheimer, J. & Gentzel Sandberg, K. (2017). *Nu. Strategisk improvisation för effektiv kommunikation.* Stockholm: Roos & Tegner.

Falkheimer, J. & Gentzel Sandberg, K. (2019). *Nu. Strategisk improvisation – ledarskap för samhällsaktörer.* Stockholm: Roos & Tegner.

March, J. (1991). *Exploration and exploitation in organizational learning.* Organization Science, Vol. 1, No. 2, pp. 71–87.

Steiber, A. & Alänge, S. (2013). *Do TQM principles need to change? Learning from a comparison to Google Inc.* Total Quality Management, Vol. 24, No. 1, pp. 48–61.

STORY

The power of nature and the smallness of man

SWEDEN. THE ISLAND OF GOTLAND IN THE MIDDLE of the Baltic Sea. Midsummer night. The community centre in the parish Burs. A play about the power of nature and the smallness of man in nature. Director Johan Paulsen:

We were supposed to stage Göran Palm's play *Sit Down Tragedy* at Stockholm City Theatre during the fall. The well-known Swedish actor Helge Skoog was set to perform the monologue, and I was the director. The play explores the power of nature, our relationship with it, and our impact on the Earth. Written in blank verse, it contains fantastic Shakespearean-level reasoning about how humans attempt to connect with nature but never truly succeed.

In the summer, we were all on Gotland and were invited to an open rehearsal at the small village hall of Burs parish. It features a small stage, accommodates about 100 spectators, and provides the opportunity to test layouts, sound illustrations, and the format in front of a live audience.

The play was supposed to be performed on a warm July evening when a magnificent storm swept over Gotland. As so often happens, there was a power outage on the island. Everything turned pitch black – both indoors and outdoors – just as the play was about to begin.

It was impossible to use the dark stage, and of course, the microphone and speakers didn't work either. But we still decided to proceed. We moved Helge down from the stage, and the audience had to shuffle forward with their chairs as best they could. We found some candles in a storage room, and I had to explain how the stage was supposed to look and the sound of the sound illustrations.

With a storm raging outside the window, thunder, lightning, and furious rain providing the backdrop, and candles serving as the sole source of light, Helge Skoog delivered his monologue on the smallness of man in nature. Where he reflected on our shortcomings in caring for our creation and the need to acknowledge that we humans are also subject to nature's laws.

It was an impetuous moment. What arose then, in the summer storm, was something we could not have foreseen, much less planned for. It would have been much easier to cancel – yet in the theatre, we are accustomed to improvising. This time, the situation necessitated a new form, and nature's force provided a concrete framework that elevated the text and the performance to something much greater.

The play premiered at Stockholm City Theatre in the fall and was very well received. "Everyone should see it. Immediately," wrote the critic from one of Sweden's leading newspapers *Dagens Nyheter*. However, it never surpassed the greatness of that evening when it was improvised during the storm, at the community centre in Burs on Gotland.

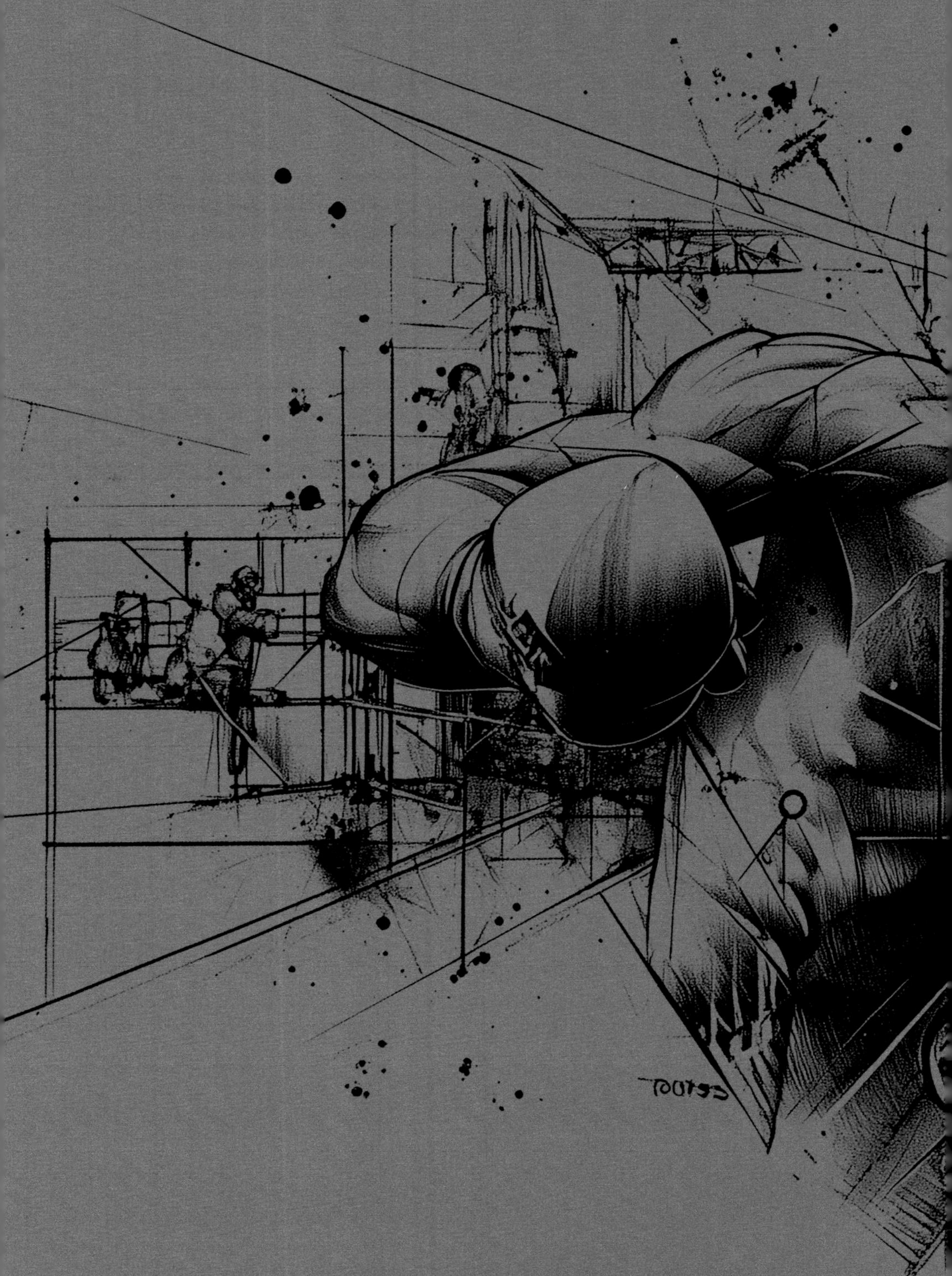

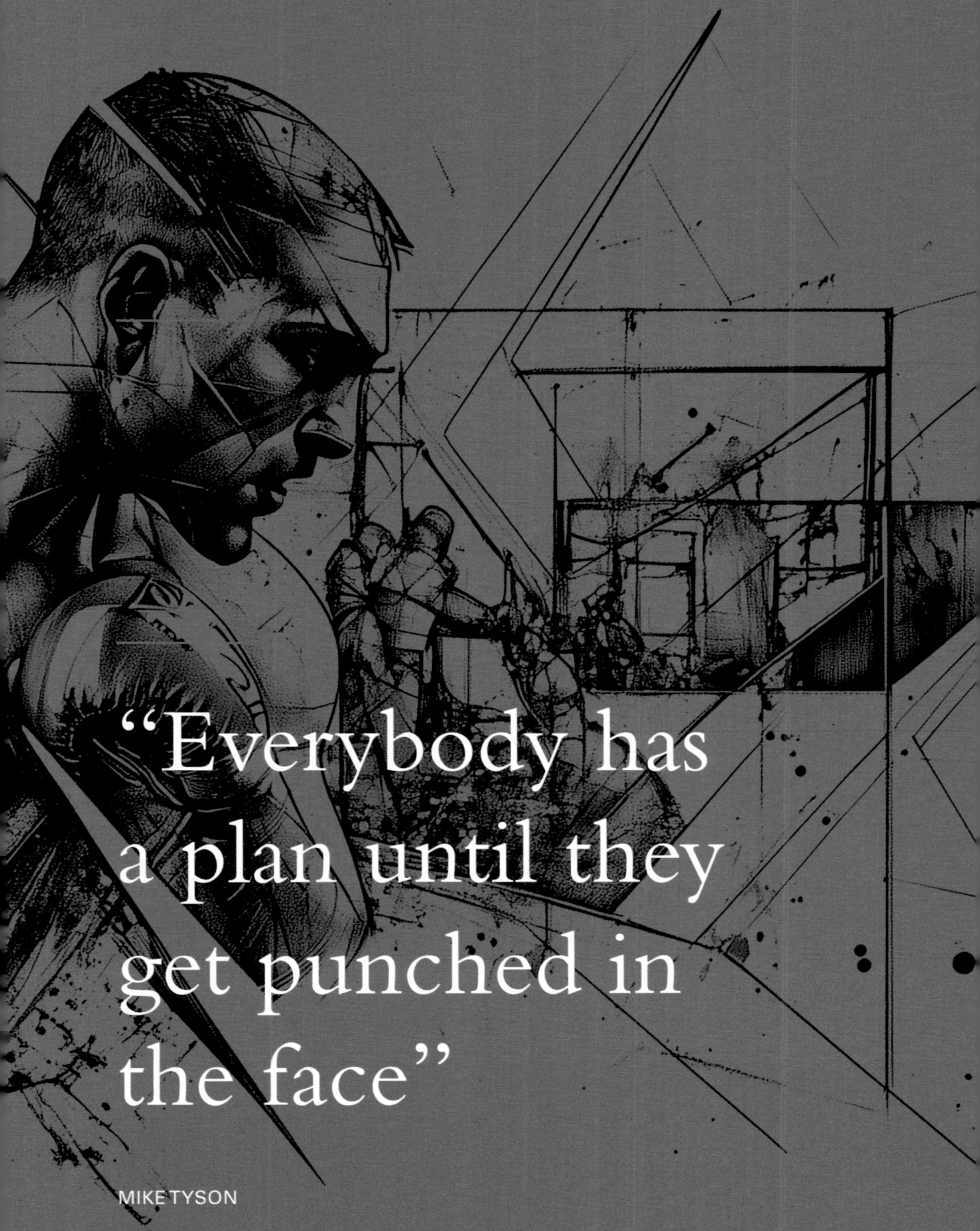

“Everybody has a plan until they get punched in the face”

MIKE TYSON

EPILOGUE

It is fair to call this book the outcome of decades of uncoordinated although systematic research as well as digested experiences from a huge variety of client assignments in all and every part of the society. Almost a testimonial text synthesising the working lives so far of the authors. And yet, it is equally true to claim that the book has a well-defined point of departure. More precisely in two books – written by Katarina Gentzel Sandberg and Jesper Falkheimer – published in Swedish in 2017 and 2019 respectively. Both rigorous inquiries, however from somewhat different perspectives, into the concept of strategic improvisation, highlighting the crucial role of communication in contemporary management.

So, is this book mainly a fusion of two other books, being translated as well, in the process of integration? Most certainly not! Several new themes are introduced although, of course, anchored in the concept of strategic improvisation. To broaden the perspectives, two authors, Hans Gennerud and Mats Tyrstrup, have contributed with insights on, for example, how strategic improvisation fits into the history of managerial practices. This included how certain changes in working life, leadership and organisational communication, can be analysed with the Management Communication Triangle introduced in this book.

In this book we have explicitly related narratives and strategic improvisation to the VUCA world. And, due to more and more pronounced VUCA features, society seems to host temporal qualities that are not necessarily consistent with a linear concept of time. Historically, management has relied heavily on distinctions such as decisions being short-, medium- or long-term in their perspectives. Implying time to unfold along a chronological dimension adding a day to a yesterday while preparing for a tomorrow. Placing reasons in the past and their consequences in the future. That is, the concept of cause and effect necessary for a main tool in managerial leadership – that of planning ahead as a mechanism for coordinating actions.

We have tried to illustrate that a short- and a long-term perspective collapse into a single focal point in situations calling for strategic improvisation. Strategy as a broadly defined course of possible actions and improvising as the intuitively chosen one related to the immediate circumstances. In fact, writing the book has itself been the subject of narratives and strategic improvisation – being written in a few years including a global pandemic, a Russian attempt to invade Ukraine, a war in the Middle East and a Western inflation crisis driving up interest rates unpleasantly high. Not to mention the turmoil on the commodity markets, especially for food and energy due to the war. From a more local perspective of the authors, also the Swedish radical change of a 200-year-old defence policy to, jointly with Finland, becoming members of NATO for the same reason. All occasions providing a rich material for discussion leadership, narratives and strategic improvisation. And doing so at certainly a dramatic level.

New in this book is also analysing the theoretical triangle between work, organisational communication and particular versions of management. A growing amount of work by specialists has, for example, changed the content of management and reduced the power of managers. As was the case in the crafting society. However, communication is also changed, now being at the very core of value creation. Specialists create values in a context of communication and provide them to customers in a variety of ways of further communication. Much contemporary work is to an extensive degree about sense-making as well as communication related to such sense-making.

There is a movement going on making management concerned with people's mindsets rather with instructions about what to do, how and when. Mindsets concerned with what we, as a business or other operation, are doing – how, for whom and why? In other words, our raison d'être and the narratives used to communicate that raison d'être. Although many pieces have been published about sense-making, value creation and leadership, for some reasons they are mainly known among scholars. We hope to contribute to a further developed practice in the area based on an explicit recognition of sense-making and communication.

The essential role of communication in specialist services suggests narratives to be at the very core of future governance. The industry society was a numbers game. It concerned issues such as production volumes, sales growth rates and return on investments. All expressed in figures calling for mathematics as the fundamental language of management. Our claim, though, is that in a VUCA world, a strategic narrative integrates a perspective of the future with current improvised actions more easily than traditional business planning. This theme is addressed in this book and implying a change of source to be inspired from in the future of leadership.

A particular problem writing this book concerned the issue of constant change. To put it mildly – it is no news precisely! It has been pointed out for long that disruptive societal changes have bothered executives for decades. Drawing heavily on social construction in our writing and, thus, sense-making we have chosen to deal with it as a communication issue. Our claim, though, becomes that a narrative allows a broader spectrum of possible relations among circumstances and pathways for the way beyond than traditional linear managerial thinking. Further, narratives communicate with the same parts of being human as a piece of languishing music, a dramatic screenplay or the reading of a fascinating family epos unfolding over decades. Human qualities are strategic resources in the creation of value in the expert society. We hope this encourages all kinds of leaders to broaden what they include in their agendas for self-development.

Many notes, texts we tested and concepts we did not fully develop, stayed of course in our board drawers or on our hard drives. Maybe embryos to further writings. However, we decided to give a glance of some of this stuff in this postface.

We have touched upon the kind of competence necessary for leading a business in need of strategic improvisation. Storytelling and communication are obvious skills that the leadership must be extremely both familiar and comfortable with. Leadership is in many ways dependent on the ability to integrate different knowledges and perspectives. Developing a narrative and strategic improvisational mindset demands a diverse set of competences, that challenges traditional management. Innovation happens in interdisciplinary contexts. Future recruiting may very well have more in common with how students are accepted at art or stage schools than what recruitment consultants currently are offering. Perhaps suggesting a solution to a business case is replaced with being asked to write an essay. The competence angle is one we would like to have developed further. But there will always be subjects in need of more elaboration. Sometimes you need set a full stop or, perhaps a comma, to allow the publication of stuff at all.

If engineering – its logics, language, ways of reasoning etcetera – were the foundation of managerial leadership during the industrial era, the arts and humanities will guide governance approaches in the future. That is our true conviction. In fact, it already does but will increase as the VUCA world continues to evolve. In that sense, engineering has served us well giving us a material welfare unprecedented in history. It will do so also in the future, in the areas in which it is relevant as a governance approach. We hope the book contributes to a further emancipation of what is considered leadership qualities as well as development areas.

We planned to write much more about the growing importance of societal actors. By societal actors we refer to all organisations (or entities) that view themselves as part of a wider society, taking responsibility also for relations and consequences beyond the core business ones. Obviously, authorities such as Police, boards of social welfare, health authorities, and other public organisations are societal actors. They have in common their responsibilities for issues – at a societal level. Their explicit aims are to promote certain behaviours as opposed to others for some reasons less favourable. It may concern healthy behaviours, the readiness to do military services or declaring taxes honestly. Obviously, establishing narratives making sense of their areas in terms of status, vital know-how and knowledge, particular recommendations etcetera, is a main task. Their assignments being concerned with public understandings of essential parts of the society constituting their positions as essential societal actors. But even more interesting is the relevance for private companies to act as societal actors. Satisfying needs and demands of customers remains of course, however, the corporate social responsibility and sustainability movement has evolved into advocating societal actorship in its fullest sense. At least in the free world, it is practically mandatory to contribute to the transformation of society. Towards sustainability, equality and a fair distribution of welfare, as proposed in the United Nations Agenda 2030.

Typically, firms have engaged communication specialists to cope with crises. In a changing societal landscape, however, private companies must act more anticipatory. And doing so for a simple reason – to establish their narratives about who they are and how they are contributing to societal transformation. Therefore – and being part in the matter – we claim that communication strategists and agencies will increasingly often be main advisors also in companies. Management consultants, though, will work with feasibility studies of already suggested strategies and the narratives promoting these strategies.

INDEX

For Product Safety Concerns and Information please contact our EU representative GPSR@taylorandfrancis.com Taylor & Francis Verlag GmbH, Kaufingerstraße 24, 80331 München, Germany

Batch number: 10733622

Printed by Printforce, the Netherlands